THE MASTERS

THE MASTERS

All About Its History, Its Records,
Its Players, Its Remarkable Course
and Even More Remarkable
Tournament

DAWSON TAYLOR

Photography by Frank Christian

South Brunswick and New York: A. S. Barnes and Company
London: Thomas Yoseloff Ltd

© 1973 by A. S. Barnes and Co., Inc.

A. S. Barnes and Co., Inc.
Cranbury, New Jersey 08512

Thomas Yoseloff Ltd
108 New Bond Street
London W1Y OQX, England

Library of Congress Cataloging in Publication Data

Taylor, Dawson.
  The Masters.

  1. Masters Golf Tournament. 2. Augusta National
Golf Club. I. Title.
GV970.T39   796.352′74′0975864   72-6378
ISBN 0-498-01251-4
ISBN 0-498-01292-1 (pbk)

To two of the greatest gentlemen golfers of all time, the late
Mr. Robert Tyre Jones, Jr., and *Mr. Clifford Roberts,*
whose good taste and intelligence have made
the Masters what it is today,
the finest golf tournament in the world.

Printed in the United States of America

Contents

Preface

How This Book Came To Be Written

I am a true golf fanatic. I love the game of golf, and I love great golf courses. I have been playing "the gentlemen's game" for more than 43 years with more or less success. My game is a respectable one with scores usually in the mid-seventies so that when I play an especially difficult course such as Pine Valley or the Augusta National Golf Club I try to break 80 (and sometimes don't!).

For a long time, I have played what I call "imaginary golf" when I could not actually play a particular course. I remember walking famous Oakmont outside of Pittsburgh one year in February when there was an inch of snow on the ground. It didn't really matter. I knew, in my mind's eye, where my drives would go, what trouble I would get into and how I would birdie the short uphill 4-par seventeenth hole to "save the round."

Then, about eight years ago, I was fortunate enough to be invited to join a fine group of golfers, gentlemen all, who were going on a jaunt to Scotland and Ireland. We played many of the famous courses—Turnberry, Troon, Carnoustie, St. Andrews, Portmarnock and others equally as renowned. One of our players, Mr. Herbert Trapp, had the thrill of an ace or hole-in-one at Dollymount or Royal Dublin. I arranged for a photograph of the group with Herb holding up the hole-in-one ball in triumph. The photographer was

Mr. David Cowie of the *Dundee Courier and Inquirer.* I asked Mr. Cowie if he would follow my round of golf the next day at St. Andrews and photograph my shots from some of the famous "hallowed" places. He would. He came the next day and the result was an unusual album of sequential photographs of myself and of some of the rest of our party playing the Old Course at St. Andrews. In particular, there were some very unusual sequences taken of searches in the gorse and heather, of striking the newly found ball and then searching for it again a few feet ahead where it had once more disappeared from view. There was one interesting photograph of my own explosion shot from "Shell" bunker over "Strath" bunker at the famous eleventh hole where the great "Bobby" Jones "picked up," certain that he had blown himself right out of the 1921 British Open tournament with a bad 6 or 7 on that hole after a first-nine score of 41 strokes.

These photographs proved to be a great consolation and pleasure to me later on, especially in the wintertime, when they could be reviewed and the game replayed mentally. I began to call this pastime "imaginary golf."

Then, in 1966, I was privileged to be invited to attend the Masters tournament at Augusta National Golf Club at Augusta, Georgia. This happened through Mr. John Walter, great sports writer of the *Detroit News* who knew Mr. Clifford Roberts, Tournament Chairman and one of the founders of the club along with Mr. Robert T. Jones, Jr.

I knew nothing about the protocol of viewing the golf course but I did know that security is very high at Augusta National. There are hundreds of Pinkerton guards to see that the gallery does not put a foot where it should not. I did not know whether I would be able to get permission to photograph the golf course from the golfer's-eye view as I wanted to do for my own game of "imaginary golf" at the Masters. I was aware that on the day before the Masters tournament starts, a 3-par competition is carried out on the delightful hilly little 3-par course adjacent to the "big" course. I surmised that galleries would be primarily interested in following the play at this tournament. I was right. I therefore arrived at the main course at noon of Wednesday, April 6, 1966, and found that the players' practice rounds were just finishing and that the course itself would be closed to players and spectators at 2:00 P.M. in order to put the final touches on the greens and fairways for the start of play the next day.

So, I had two hours to myself and without any interference from the guards watching around each green I proceeded to photograph the view from each tee and then, having driven my imaginary ball to a particular spot (always in the fairway that day!), I would snap the view from there to the hole or green in question. By the twelfth hole, time caught up with me and I was told by a most polite Pinkerton guard that I must leave the course since it was being closed then. I did so but managed to photograph the seventeenth and eighteenth holes on the way in to the clubhouse.

The photographs that resulted from this adventure proved to be delightfully useful for my mental game in the subsequent months when I "played" Augusta National Golf Club in my mind. But I had to admit that the photographs—beautiful as they were in color—were amateurish. It was clear that I needed a professional photographer to do the photographic work properly and completely, to get every nuance of the course: fairway shots, trouble shots, bunker shots, Rae's creek and its rocks. In short, I wanted to do the job to perfection. In the meantime, I had spoken to Mr. Thomas

Yoseloff of A. S. Barnes and Company, Inc., who had published my first three books, *The Secret of Bowling Strikes, The Secret of Holing Putts* (with Horton Smith), and *The Making of the Pope*. He agreed that my idea for a book concerning the Masters was feasible and gave his permission for me to proceed to bring it to completion. However, his first reaction to my proposed "Imaginary Golf at the Masters" was, "I think that you have more of a book in prospect than you realize. Why don't you see if you can get permission to research the records of the past Masters tournaments, get some historical photographs and broaden the appeal of the book by getting the stories of the victories and failures of the stars of golf—Jones, Hogan, Nelson, Palmer, Player, and Nicklaus?"

I met Mr. Clifford Roberts on April 14, 1971, submitted the idea of the book to him and, gracious gentleman that he is, Mr. Roberts granted permission for me to have access to the tournament records and said that I should come back several weeks later to begin work on the book. He suggested that to do the job properly I should play the magnificent Augusta National Golf Club course myself. Then, in writing the book subsequently, I would better understand the problems the players encounter in the tournament. Mr. Philip Wahl, Club Manager, and equally gracious as Mr. Roberts, suggested that he would be pleased to assign one of the famous caddies in white coveralls for my round and said that he would even arrange to put one of the distinctive name tags on the caddy's back.

May 4, 1971, dawned bright and clear with the temperatures in the high 60s and low 70s. My photographer was Mr. Frank Christian, official photographer on the Masters, following in the footsteps of his father, who was named the original official photographer in 1934. It was a delightful experience for this "true golfer" to play the Augusta National Golf course. My score that day shall forever remain a secret between Leon, my wonderful caddy, and me. Frank Christian and I were allowed to go into the locker rooms, trophy rooms, and places on the golf course where gallery members may never go. More than three hundred photographs were taken that day. Mrs. Wilda Gwin, Mr. Roberts' Executive Secretary, most kindly opened up the tournament record files to me. She had copies of the only tournament programs ever issued, those of 1934 and 1935. There was a wealth of information in them alone, particularly the comments of Dr. Alister MacKenzie regarding the construction of the course and the similarity of several Augusta holes to famous holes in Great Britain and Scotland. In the Frank Christian Studio files there were many historical black and white photographs as well as another three hundred color transparencies of the play in earlier Masters tournaments. Soon it was obvious that the book should become a complete tournament record of all the Masters tournaments embellished by historical photographs and by color drawings of the holes on the golf course. Fortunately, a recent topographical survey of the terrain had been made. This was made available to me and, subsequently, Kenneth Seaquist, a fine landscape architect, drew the beautiful hole-by-hole layouts that you find in this book following the tournament records. Those golfer-readers who wish to play "Imaginary Golf at the Masters" should be able to do so by following the hole-by-hole drawings in plan layout and in "profile" layout.

Countless hours of research and study were spent in the microfilm library of the *New York Times* in my attempt to recreate the scene and the drama of the many past Masters tournaments. This I hope I have been able to do in the "capsule histories" of the Masters.

I hope that I have been able to convey a feeling of awe at the magnificent beauty of the course and its extreme difficulty, and also a sense of reverence and admiration for the "mystique" of the Masters, the tastefulness and good sense of the people who run the tournament so smoothly, so efficiently, that without any question of doubt it is the most enjoyable golf tournament held anywhere in the world.

Dawson Taylor

Acknowledgments

I should like to take this opportunity to thank Mr. Clifford Roberts, Chairman of the Masters Tournament Committee of the Augusta National Golf Club, for his kind permission to proceed with this book and his cooperation throughout the year and a half of its making. Mrs. Wilda Gwin, Mr. Roberts's Executive Secretary, has also been most helpful in uncovering so many of the facts and figures concerning past Masters tournaments.

Further credits should be given to Mr. Philip Wahl, Manager of the Augusta National Golf Club for his help in the photographic arrangements and for obtaining the topographical information which adds so much to this book; to Mr. John Walter, fine sports writer of the *Detroit News,* for his suggestions and encouragement on this project; to Mr. Glynn ("Bud") Harvey of the Professional Golf Association for the use of historical photographs in the P.G.A. archives and for his encouragement; to Doubleday and Company for their permission to reprint excerpts from the writings of Robert T. Jones, Jr.; to Prentice-Hall, Inc., for their permission to reprint excerpts from *Advanced Golf,* by Cary Middlecoff; to A. S. Barnes and Company, Inc., for permission to reprint excerpts from *The Secret of Holing Putts* by Horton Smith and Dawson Taylor, and for use of *The Encyclopedia of Golf* for assorted facts and figures; to Tom Flaherty for permission to use excerpts from his book, *The Masters;* to the *New York Times* and its great golf writers, W. D. Richardson and Lincoln Werden, and their coverage of the Masters tournaments; to *Sports Illustrated* for its equally fine golf reportage.

Photographic Credits:
Smith, Hogan, Demaret picture: C. E. Engelbrecht, Sparta, N. J.
Henry Picard picture: Bert and Richard Morgan Studio, Palm Beach, Florida
Ben Hogan, Robert T. Jones, Jr., Clifford Roberts: P.G.A. of America
Sam Snead, 1949 Masters: Augusta National Golf Club, George Schaeffer, Augusta, Ga.

Comments on the Masters

The Masters is a distinctive golfing classic. To me, the Augusta National course has character, individuality and personality. It is one of the few courses that really presents two games on most every hole—one game to reach the greens and another to figure the ever challenging contours after reaching them. Many courses provide interesting shots to the greens but very dull or mechanical putting after the green has been reached. I feel "contour" is the best feature of the course—placing tee shots in the best places to simplify the shots to the greens and figuring the slopes and speed of the large and undulating putting surfaces.

Horton Smith
Masters Champion 1934 and 1936
Member of Hall of Fame of Golf

THE MASTERS

1
The Beginning

In 1930, Robert T. Jones, Jr. in the eyes of the American public held a place of esteem second only to the immortal Babe Ruth. In fact, it might be said that "Bobby" Jones (all his life "Bob" Jones hated that diminutive nickname and his friends never used it) brought the game of golf to the attention of millions of persons who either had never heard of the game before or, having heard of it, dismissed it as an effete game for rich men's sons.

Jones had had a remarkable career in golf. Even as a youngster of fourteen he had qualified for the United States Open—the toughest tournament in U. S. Golf. He had won everything there was to win in golf by late 1929, so that when he won all four of the important championships in 1930—the British Amateur, the British Open, the United States Open, and finally the United States Amateur —he had accomplished what came to be called "The Grand Slam of Golf." When he returned to America after winning the last British championship he was given a ticker-tape procession down New York City's Fifth Avenue—the welcome of an Eisenhower returning triumphant from the war.

Bob Jones had done everything he had set his mind and body to do in the world of competitive golf, but he was tired from fourteen years of the battle: tired of the sinking feeling in the pit of his stomach as he stepped onto the next first tee of a championship course; tired of not eating because he couldn't eat during important matches; tired of the adulation of the crowds who would not allow him a private game of golf for his own pleasure.

So in 1930 Bob Jones announced that he would no longer engage in competitive golf, but would retire to his law practice and business at his home in Atlanta. The American public was amazed at his decision, but as time went on, it began to see how right the decision had been. Perhaps Babe Ruth should have quit baseball immediately after hitting his record 60 home runs in one season. Later on, didn't Joe Di Maggio model his own career after Bob Jones?

So, Bob Jones did quit the competitive trail and played "friendly golf" with people whose company he enjoyed. He could now give instructions in golf, something he had dared not do as an amateur. The finest golf instructional movies came from Warner Brothers Films as a result of Bob Jones's knowledge and love of the game. He looked into the problem of better club design. His own set had been a conglomerate clutch of "all different" clubs, with weights and balances that did not agree with one another. Jones was sure that he could help design a better golf club and he did. The A. C. Spalding Co. brought out a set of Jones-designed golf clubs and sold them by the millions to the golfers of America. After all, hadn't the great Bobby Jones designed them?

Finally it came time for another venture Bob Jones had had in mind for many years. He wanted to help design and build a golf course with all the delights and challenges, the pleasures and travails, of the many fine courses he had played in his long career. He would find a choice piece of rolling countryside in Atlanta or near to it, and there he would build a "golfer's Paradise" for himself and for his friends to enjoy. At last he would be able to play that private friendly game without the mob being on his heels beseeching him for autographs at each successive tee.

At this point in Bob Jones's life there occurred a most marvelous melding of his great talents and experience with those of a successful Wall Street banker named Clifford Roberts. The two men had met several years before at a golf tournament. Roberts occasionally visited in Augusta, Georgia. Bob Jones's wife had been born in Augusta. Cliff Roberts was aware of 365 acres of beautiful rolling Georgia pinelands that might fit into Bob Jones's golf-course-building plans. The property had been in the hands of a famous horticulturist and nursery owner, a Belgian Baron named Prosper Jules Alphonse Berckmans. Although we are getting ahead of the story a bit, later on when the beautiful Augusta National opened its doors in 1932, P. J. A. Berckmans's son (whose name was identical with his father's) was General Manager of the club and his brother Alphonse Berckmans was its Treasurer.

The Berckmans family had moved to Augusta in 1857, after having left Europe for political reasons. P. J. A. Berckmans, Sr. was a scholar, a horticulturist, a landscape architect, a botanist, and a nursery man. In Augusta he established the foremost nursery in the United States of America. In recognition of his remarkable work in horticulture, Mr. Berckmans was honored by many societies in Europe and America. The University of Georgia bestowed on him a degree of Master of Science. He originated and disseminated hundreds of species of flowers, shrubs, and trees. It is very probable that without his imagination and talent the American South as we know it now would not have been so beautified with azaleas and camellias,

with peach and jasmine trees. In the catalogue of Berckmans's nursery for 1861, there were 1,300 varieties of pears, 900 of apples, 300 of grapes, and over 100 each of azaleas and camellias.

It was to this magnificent spot that Robert T. Jones and Clifford Roberts came. Accompanying them was Alfred Bourne of the Singer Sewing Machine Company who had a winter home in Augusta. Incidentally, the explanation for one's having a "winter home" in Augusta is that Atlanta is 1050 feet above sea level to Augusta's 162. Winters are cold in Atlanta, less severe in Augusta.

Jones has recorded in the following words what he felt, as he turned off the highway and rode down the long archway of magnolias to the manor house: "I stood at the top of the hill before that fine old house and looked at the wide stretch of land rolling down the slope before me. It was cleared land for the most part, and you could take in the whole vista all the way down to Rae's creek. I knew instantly it was the kind of terrain I had always hoped to find. I had been told, of course, about the marvelous trees and plants, but I was still unprepared for the great bonus of beauty Fruitlands offered. Frankly, I was overwhelmed by the exciting possibilities of a golf course set in the midst of such a nursery."

Next, the organization of the new golf club membership was established. Clifford Roberts and Robert Jones had many friends throughout the country, "true golfers"—that is, gentlemen who would appreciate and enjoy the kind of golf course and golf club membership the two entrepreneurs were envisioning. They sought and obtained a cosmopolitan group of members.

The program published in 1934 for the "First Annual Invitation Tournament" had a section devoted to "Some of the members of Augusta National Golf Club" along with their portraits. Among the names were Edward F. Hutton, the stockbroker of New York City; Eugene G. Grace of the Steelmakers in Bethlehem, Pennsylvania; L. B. Maytag, industrialist of Newton, Iowa; the sports writer, Grantland Rice, and many other equally as prominent gentlemen and substantial businessmen. Only thirty members were to be allowed from Augusta itself. Truly, this club would be a "National" golf club in every sense of the word.

Robert T. Jones, Jr. had always admired the golf architecture of the famous Scot, Dr. Alister Mac-Kenzie. Dr. MacKenzie was the overwhelming choice to design the new course and after accepting the challenge set about laying out the course in the spring of 1931.

Both Jones and MacKenzie wanted to construct a challenging golf course that would take the greatest possible advantage of the natural terrain and the natural beauty of the nursery acreage. Jones and MacKenzie were great believers in the principle of "Strategic design" of a golf course. That is, let the player judge his own capabilities on any given day, and give him one or even two alternate "routes" or methods of attack on par. If the player felt strong he should be encouraged to "cut the dog-leg" and be rewarded, after a successful shot, with a simpler shot to birdie territory than, say, the player who skirted trouble, "played it safe," and thus would be left with a longer, more difficult shot onto the green. Here were two golf "experts"—MacKenzie by training and experience, Jones with less formal training but even greater golf playing experience and basic intuition concerning the rightness and wrongness of a golf hole layout. They decided to reward the player in pro-

portion to the type of golf shot required of him and how well that shot was played.

Jones planned the Augusta course as a "wide-open" one, because he wanted to accommodate the average golfer. So, to make things more difficult for the good golfer, the hole itself was made more difficult. This was done by placing the flagsticks in more difficult and demanding positions—perhaps just over an upslope on a green, perhaps tucked in neatly behind a front guarding bunker. In addition, the speed of the greens was increased by cutting them closely with the mowers. The cups were then narrowed and sometimes it was said that the only opening to the hole was in the dead center of the cup. The greens, too, were maintained in a firm condition so that the approach shot that did not have underspin on it might hit once on the green and then continue to roll and roll, even off the green at the rear.

The greens at Augusta National were designed to be large and with large and small undulations in them. The combination of speed in putting and the subtle slopes proved to be very difficult for all but the keenest putting touch. Truly it would be said only a "Master" would win a tournament at this golf course.

2

Jones on the Design of the Course

The Augusta National Golf Club itself was born of very modest aspirations to begin with. Clifford Roberts had been coming to Augusta for some years as a seasonably regular winter visitor. He and I were close friends of Walton H. Marshall of the Vanderbilt Hotel in New York City, who also operated the Bon Air Vanderbilt in Augusta during the winter season. We were also patrons of both Marshall hotels.

Living in Atlanta only a short distance away, I had come to Augusta often over a period of years for friendly golf and an occasional charity match. I also played in the Southeastern Open Tournament over the country club and Forest Hills courses in Augusta during the early part of 1930. I had always been impressed by the fact that, especially during the winter season, golf courses around Augusta were considerably better conditioned than courses near Atlanta, and since at that time we were doomed to coarse Bermuda grass for putting greens in the summer, it was in winter golf that our best hope lay.

In any event, when Cliff came to Atlanta during the late fall of 1930 to suggest to me that I join him in organizing a club and building a golf course near Augusta, I found myself in a very receptive frame of mind.

The attractive aspects of the proposal were somewhat as follows: Augusta was well known to me as a resort area and a pleasant setting for golf during the winter months. Cliff and I had a number of friends among the permanent and winter residents there who could be counted on to form a nucleus around which to build our club. I felt that the financing of such a project would be infinitely more likely to succeed in Augusta than in Atlanta.

Secondly, I was acutely aware of the fact that my native Southland, especially my own neighborhood, had very few, if any, golf courses of championship quality. The prospect of myself building a course according to the high standards of excellence I would set, based on what I considered to be a very wide experience in the game, was most intriguing. I truly regarded it as an opportunity to make a contribution to golf in my own section of the country, as well as to give expression to my own very definite ideas about golf-course design.

Thirdly, the piece of ground available, as described by Cliff and as later confirmed by me in a personal visit, seemed ideally suited to the purpose Cliff was suggesting. In brief, the dream was completely enthralling, especially at a time when I was, I suppose, flushed with success and already deeply involved in enough golfing projects to preclude, at least for many years, my taking any serious interest in other activities.

As the name implies, the new club was set up on a national basis. We planned to have only a small group of local members upon whom we could rely for help in the day-to-day administration of the club's affairs. Our aim was to develop a golf course and a retreat of such nature, and of such excellence, that men of some means and devoted to the game of golf might find the club worthwhile as an extra luxury where they might visit and play with kindred spirits from other parts of the nation. This policy has never been changed, and I am happy to be able to say that the club apparently has adequately fulfilled this mission.

In this view, of course, the all-important thing was to be the golf course, I shall never forget my first visit to the property which is now the Augusta National. The long lane of magnolias through which we approached was beautiful. The old manor house with its cupola and walls of masonry two feet thick was charming. The rare trees and shrubs of the old nursery were enchanting. But when I walked out on the grass terrace under the big trees behind the house and looked down over the property, the experience was unforgettable. It seemed that this land had been lying here for years just waiting for someone to lay a golf course upon it. Indeed, it even looked as though it were already a golf course, and I am sure that one standing today where I stood on this first visit, on the terrace overlooking the practice putting green, sees the property almost exactly as I saw it then. The grass of the fairways and greens is greener, of course, and some of the pines are a bit larger but the broad expanse of the main body of the property lay at my feet then just as it does now.

I still like to sit on this terrace, and can do so for hours at a time, enjoying the beauty of this panorama.

With this sort of land, of a soft, gentle rather than spectacular beauty, it was especially appropriate that we chose Dr. Alister Mackenzie to design our course. For it was essential to our requirements that we build a course within the

capacity of the average golfer to enjoy. This did not mean that the design would be insipid, for our players were expected to be sophisticated. They would demand interesting, lively golf, but would not endure a course which kept them constantly straining for distance and playing out of sand.

There was much conversation at the time to the effect that Mackenzie and I expected to reproduce in their entirety holes of famous courses around the world where I had played in competitions. This was, at best, a bit naive, because to do such a thing, we would have had literally to alter the face of the earth. It was to be expected, of course, that the new layout would be strongly influenced by holes which either Mackenzie or I had admired, but it was only possible that we should have certain features of these holes in mind and attempt to adapt them to the terrain with which we were working.

I think Mackenzie and I managed to work as a completely sympathetic team. Of course, there was never any question that he was the architect and I his advisor and consultant. No man learns to design a golf course simply by playing golf, no matter how well. But it happened that both of us were extravagant admirers of the Old Course at St. Andrews and we both desired as much as possible to simulate seaside conditions insofar as the differences in turf and terrain would allow.

Mackenzie was very fond of expressing his creed as a golf-course architect by saying that he tried to build courses for the "most enjoyment for the greatest number." This happened to coincide completely with my own view. It had seemed to me that too many courses I had seen had been constructed with an eye to difficulty alone, and that in the effort to construct an exacting course which would thwart the expert, the average golfer who paid the bills was entirely overlooked. Too often the worth of a layout seemed to be measured by how successfully it had withstood the efforts of professionals to better its par or to lower its record.

The first purpose of any golf course should be to give pleasure, and that to the greatest possible number of players, without respect to their capabilities. As far as possible, there should be presented to each golfer an interesting problem which will test him without being so impossibly difficult that he will have little chance of success. There must be something to do, but that something must always be within the realm of reasonable accomplishment.

From the standpoint of the inexpert player, there is nothing so disheartening as the appearance of a carry which is beyond his best effort and which offers no alternative route. In such a situation, there is nothing for the golfer to do, for he is given no opportunity to overcome his deficiency in length by either accuracy or judgment.

With respect to the employment of hazards off the tee and through the green, the doctor and I agreed that two things were essential. First, there must be a way for those unwilling to attempt the carry; and second, there must be a definite reward awaiting the man who makes it. Without the alternative route the situation is unfair. Without the reward it is meaningless.

There are two ways of widening the gap between a good tee shot and a bad one. One is to inflict a severe and immediate punishment on a bad shot, to place its perpetrator in a bunker or in some other trouble which will demand the sacrifice of a stroke in recovering. The other is to reward the good shot by making the second shot simpler in proportion to the excellence of the first. The reward may be of any nature, but it is more commonly one of four—a better view of the green, an easier angle from which to attack a slope, an open approach past guarding hazards, or even a better run to the tee shot itself. But the elimination of purely punitive hazards provides an opportunity for the player to retrieve his situation by an exceptional second shot.

A course which is constructed with these principles in view must be interesting, because it will offer problems which a man may attempt according to his ability. It will never become hopeless for the duffer, nor fail to concern and interest the expert. And it will be found, like old St. Andrews, to become more delightful the more it is studied and played.

We try very hard in Augusta to avoid placing meaningless bunkers on the course. Some of the natural hazards are severe, but usually so for the ambitious player. Possibly the dearth of bunkers on the course is a feature most commented upon

by visitors. Yet there are some which perhaps could be dispensed with, except that they are in use to protect players from more dire consequences. Occasionally a bunker may be used to stop a ball from running into a hazard of a more serious nature.

I have already said that 1931 was a very bad year in which to start a golf club. The depression got worse instead of better. The early years of the club were not easy from an operating standpoint.

The golf course, on the other hand, gave every indication of fulfilling our ambitions for it in a most gratifying way. We very soon became convinced of the soundness of the basic conceptions upon which the course had been built. Most important of all to me was confirmation of my hope that during the spring months a combination of Bermuda base and Italian-rye surface could provide as good putting as was to be found anywhere. For the first time I became aware that championship golf could be played in the South.

Somewhere during the second year of the existence of the golf course in its completed form, and from somewhere within the hard core of faithful who had accepted responsibility for the direction of the club, there came the suggestion that we try to get the National Open Championship for our club. We had many conversations on the subject among ourselves, and with officials of the United States Golf Association.

The idea was regarded among all of us as not entirely without merit, but in the end, enough objections were found to cause us all to agree that the project was not feasible, the most important opposing reason being that the championship would have to be played during the early spring instead of, as customarily during the month of June or the first half of July.

These conversations were really the beginnings of the Masters Tournament, because from them Clifford Roberts came up with the idea that we might stage a tournament of our own. In this way we might just as well demonstrate the virtues of the kind of golf course we had created and, at the same time, bring to Augusta and the adjoining section an annual golfing event which would give our people the opportunity to see the world's best players in action on a first-class golf course.

It was Cliff also who persuaded me that the tournament could be set apart from the rest of those springing up as fixtures on the winter circuit, by casting me in the role of host and building the tournament around this as my one appearance in competition. I must confess that the prospect of annually entertaining my old playmates and the later arrivals in the upper crust of competitive golf was quite attractive.

From the very beginning we planned the tournament on an invitational basis. As president of the club, it was to be my privilege to invite a limited number of men I considered likely to grace the tournament because of their past accomplishments in the game, their present stature, their promise, or even upon my own feeling of friendship for them.

We have ever since retained the invitational character of the tournament, but it took no time at all for us to discover that on the original basis, I and others in the club's official family had let ourselves in for a considerable amount of embarrassment so long as we should construct the invitation list on any such free and easy basis. Our club's facilities, which are still not spacious, were at that time stringent indeed. It was an utter impossi-

bility to include everyone whom I might wish to invite for any reason, and still keep the field down to manageable numbers. It became obvious that the only possible solution was the one which we followed namely to adopt a definite set of qualifications which a player must meet in order to be considered for an invitation. And obviously, too, this set of qualifications, after its adoption for any one tournament, had to be so rigid that even I was not able to deviate from it.

The first tournament was called the Augusta National Invitation Tournament, but, even before its playing, Cliff had begun to think and talk of it as the Masters. I have occasionally forgotten this fact, but having had my memory refreshed, I remember very well that I resisted for a time the application of this name to our tournament. When Cliff suggested it, I vetoed it on the basis that it was a title entirely too presumptuous for us to apply to a tournament of our creation. I am not so certain that our ends have not been served best by this reluctance. I think the tournament is now quite well entitled to be called the Masters, because it has continued to assemble those who are entitled to be called masters of the game.

3

A Discussion of the Augusta National Course

By DR. ALISTER MACKENZIE

In writing of the course I designed at Augusta, Georgia, for the Augusta National Golf Club, I want to emphasize the importance of the part played by Robert T. Jones, Jr., in working out the plans. Bob is not only a student of golf, but of golf courses as well and while I had known him for years, I was amazed at his knowledge and clear recollection of almost all of the particularly famous golf holes in England and Scotland, as well as in America. Partly by reason of his college training in engineering, his suggestions were not only unique and original but were also practical.

As President of the Augusta National Golf Club, Robert T. Jones, Jr. has been an active leader in all matters pertaining to designing, construction and organization. He has assumed the major responsibility in this effort, which we call an attempt to build "the ideal golf course."

What is the "ideal golf course"? Bob Jones and I found ourselves in complete agreement on these essentials:

1. A really great course must be pleasurable to the greatest possible number.
2. It must require strategy as well as skill or it cannot be enduringly interesting.
3. It must give the average player a fair chance and at the same time require the utmost from the expert who tries for sub-par scores.
4. All natural beauty should be preserved, natural hazards utilized and a minimum of artificiality introduced.

In constructing Augusta National, we had plenty of land, towering pine forests, a large variety of other trees, beautiful shrubbery, streams of water, a mildly rolling terrain of great variety, a rich soil for growing good fairway grass and a naturally beautiful setting from an architectural standpoint.

As you may know, the property was originally settled in 1857, by a Belgian nobleman named Prosper Jules Alphonse Berckmans. He was an ardent horticulturist and in this property he indulged his hobby to the limit of his resources. There are azaleas in abundance and a great variety of small plants, shrubbery and hedges, even a real cork tree. There are scores of camellia bushes that are so well grown in size now that they are really trees. Most impressive of all sights is the ancient double row of magnolia trees planted before the Civil War. They are said to be the finest in the South and stand like sentinels along the driveway entrance into the "Golfer's Paradise."

Now to get back to our golf course. It has been

suggested that it was our intention at Augusta to produce copies of the most famous golf holes in the world. Any attempt of this kind could only result in failure. It may be possible to reproduce a famous picture, but the charm of a golf hole may be dependent upon a background of sand dunes, trees, or even mountains miles away. A copy without surroundings might create an unnatural appearance and cause a feeling of irritation, instead of charm. On the other hand, it is well to have a mental picture of the world's outstanding holes and to use this knowledge in reproducing their finest features, and perhaps even improving upon them.

At Augusta, we tried to produce eighteen ideal holes, not copies of classical holes, but holes that embodied their finest golfing features, with other features suggested by the nature of the terrain. We hope that our accomplishments at Augusta will be of such unique character that these holes will be looked upon as classics in themselves.

An aerial view in the 1940s of the 9th and 18th holes.
Notice the automobiles between the 18th fairway and
the 10th fairway, the parking in the practice grounds
and the absence of the 3 par course.

4
What Is "Tradition"?

It has often been said that the Masters Tournament has great "tradition" surrounding it. This is very true. A visitor to Augusta in April who partakes of the scene for a day or more comes away filled with an understanding of how "tradition" can affect and increase greatly the enjoyment of the players and the gallery who are jointly participating in this remarkable tournament.

The word "tradition" itself comes from the Latin *trado*, to hand over. The meaning of the word applicable to the Masters refers to handing down "an inheritance to posterity"—a set of customs, a way of doing things, especially at the Augusta National, in a gentlemanly fashion.

It is the tradition of last year's Masters Champion helping the new champion into his green "Masters" coat.

It is the sentiment expressed in having Freddie McLeod and Jock Hutchinson, venerable open champions, always the first twosome to begin the tournament, precisely on the stroke of the starting hour the morning of the first day.

It is the absence of commercialism in the beautifully printed, starting-time schedules handed out generously and free to the guests at the Masters.

It is the lightness and easygoing nature of the Three-Par Tournament on the Wednesday before the Masters begins, a delightful warmup for the

The stentorian-voiced Ralph Hutchinson, veteran field announcer of good and bad scores.

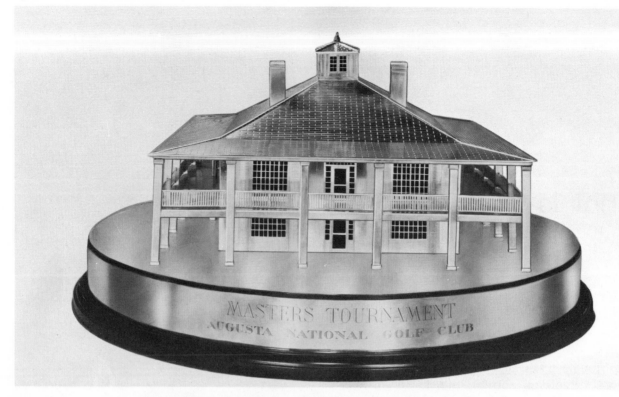

The Trophy of Augusta National Golf Club for The Masters

Designed by Mr. Gordon Lang of Spaulding and Company, Jewelers of Chicago, Illinois, this trophy was created in 1961 to be the permanent trophy of the Masters Tournament. It contains 900 individual pieces, was executed in England by the silversmiths, and assembled in America. Other famous trophies which have been made by Spaulding and Company are the World Team Championship, The United States Amateur Championship trophy, and the America's Cup trophy. A sterling silver miniature replica of the large trophy is presented to each Masters champion as a symbol of his victory. The ebony base of the large trophy is 4 feet in diameter, and the sterling silver band around the base is 9 feet, 6 inches in length.

The Trophy Room

At Augusta National Golf Club there is a modest trophy room at the south end of the clubhouse. There are two glass cases, lighted from within, that display the set of golf clubs used by Robert T. Jones, Jr., in winning his four championships in 1930. There are also some famous golf clubs and golf balls used by Masters champions in their victories.

Horton Smith's putter of 1934 and 1936 is in the case. It's a very long blade putter with a built-up heel. The 4-wood Gene Sarazen used for his "double eagle" on #15 in 1935 is there, once and for all disproving the many statements that he had used a "spoon" or 3-wood for the shot. There is a 1-iron Byron Nelson used in 1937 and 1942, and a 4-wood Ben Hogan used in 1951 and 1953. Interestingly, both these clubs have the "all-weather" grips on them, the rubber impregnated with cord so as to give a better grip in rainy weather.

The putter Cary Middlecoff used in his victory of 1955 is there, a mallet-headed model with several holes drilled in the bottom to lighten the weight. Gene Sarazen's "double-eagle" ball is also there on a little pedestal. He used a Wilson #3 with two tiny flags on it, one in red, one in blue.

Ben Hogan's ball from 1953 when he scored the record low score of 274 is on its little stand, too. Ben used a 90 compression Titleist (Red #5). It is said that Ben Hogan never played a ball in a round unless he had tried it out beforehand on the practice range.

A view of the small crowd at the 9th and 18th greens
in the 1930s.

A crowd around the 9th green in the 30s.

players and spectators in more than one sense of the word.

It is Mr. Clifford Roberts himself in an electric cart with an assistant personally checking the farthest reaches of the golf course to make sure everything is running in its accustomed smooth fashion.

It is the genial caddy in spotless white overalls leaping with glee when his player sinks a birdie putt.

It is the chorus of mockingbirds along with several sweet cardinals singing for love of life in the woods around the first green which has been freshly doubly mowed, and is ready for a close approach to the cup in its apparently impregnable position of difficulty.

It is the small, elite field of golfers from all over the world, every one of whom is famous either in name or by reputation to the knowledgeable spectators.

It is the young, inexperienced amateur on stage in his first major tournament with an Arnold Palmer or a Jack Nicklaus as his playing partner, dreaming of the day when he, too, will become one of the greats.

It is the standing ovation of the crowds at the 15th hole when an ancient and now fading Champion reaches the proximity of the green and makes a commendable golf shot. It is the tipped visor and smile that follows.

It is the gasp of excitement when another red number goes up on the scoreboards for a front-running leader in the field, and the equivalent gasp of amazement and disappointment when red numbers turn to green and a well-known name comes down from the "leader-board."

The crowd at the 18th green in the 1940s. One of the first scoreboard towers.

A rudimentary scoreboard in the late 30s, and the
small crowd watching the scores being posted in chalk.

A view of the crowd below the 18th green in the
early 40s.

A mint julep under the magnolia trees in the 1940s.

It is Eddie Thompson in his red announcer's jacket at the ninth green kindly informing the gallery that the next twosome will present the former Open Champion of the United States in 1947 and his partner, winner of the Azalea Open of 1972.

It is seeing a legendary international golf star such as Joe Carr of Ireland or Roberto de Vicenzo of Argentina come to life in person and seeing him "hold his own" with America's best golfers.

It is the sight of the beautiful women and their well-dressed escorts sipping mint juleps at the cafe tables under the magnolia trees on the front lawn of the clubhouse overlooking the entire golfing scene below.

It is the white dogwood, the pink azaleas, the riot of flowers, the meadowlark song, the riot of color, "the splendor, splendor everywhere."

A rare photograph of Alfred S. Bourne (left), one of the founding members of Augusta National. Otto Hackbarth (center) and Fred McLeod tied for the PGA Seniors Championship played at Augusta National in 1938. Fred won with an 80 to Otto's 82 in a bad rainstorm. The Bourne trophy was retired in 1962.

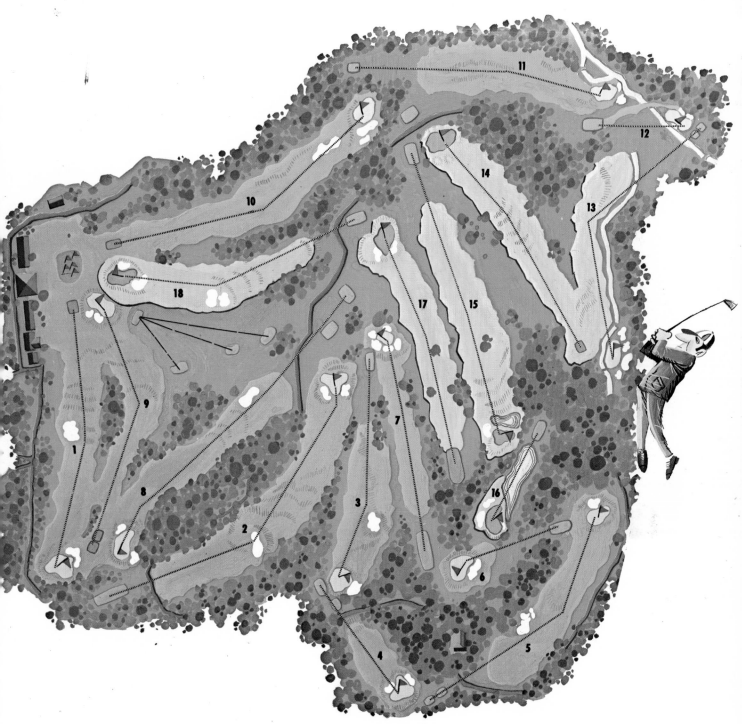

Layout of the Augusta National Golf Club.

The Masters Champions Dinner, 1968. From the left: Herman Keiser, Sam Snead, Gene Sarazen, Byron Nelson, Cary Middlecoff, Henry Picard, Jack Nicklaus, Clifford Roberts, Arnold Palmer, Ralph Guldahl, Gary Player, Claude Harmon, Art Wall, Jr., Doug Ford, Craig Wood, and Jack Burke, Jr.

Bob Goalby, left, Masters Champion of 1968 congratulates the 1969 Champion, George Archer.

The Masters Champions Dinner, 1969. From the left: Gary Player, Cary Middlecoff, Claude Harmon, Jack Nicklaus, Herman Keiser, Henry Picard, Arnold Palmer, Clifford Roberts, Bob Goalby, Gay Brewer, Jr., Byron Nelson, Gene Sarazen, Sam Snead, Jack Burke, Jr., Art Wall, Jr., Ralph Guldahl, and Doug Ford.

"The Manor House," clubhouse of the Augusta National Golf Club.

Jock Hutchinson and Freddie McLeod are given the microphone by Clifford Roberts as they prepare to tee off, as usual, as the first twosome of the Masters.

An aerial view of the Augusta National Golf Club, looking southwest.

A press conference: reporters quiz Jack Nicklaus.

The Masters Champions Dinner, 1971. From the left: Gay Brewer, Jr., Art Wall, Jr., Bob Goalby, Sam Snead, George Archer, Gene Sarazen, Gary Player, Arnold Palmer, Clifford Roberts, Billy Casper, Jr., Jack Nicklaus, Henry Picard, Byron Nelson, Ralph Guldahl, Cary Middlecoff, Herman Keiser, Doug Ford, and Claude Harmon.

Arnold Palmer drives from the 16th tee.

The scene at the first tee on opening day, 1972. In traditional fashion, Freddie McLeod and Jock Hutchinson tee off as the first twosome. McLeod, now 89 years old, won the U. S. Open in 1908. Hutchinson, 87, won the British Open in 1921, and the P. G. A. in 1920.

A crowd in the 1940s.

5

Understanding the Terrain at the Masters

You enter the Augusta National Golf Club after leaving a busy highway. At once you find yourself behind boxwood hedges that emit heavenly odors. It is here that you begin to sense the quiet and peacefulness of this wonderful club and golf course.

Twenty-five feet inside the gate you pass a gatehouse, stationed in which is a uniformed watchman who will politely ask your name, phone ahead to the clubhouse to see whether your arrival is expected, and if you are expected, will direct you to proceed the 275 yards farther ahead, where the white colonial clubhouse stands behind a circular driveway.

On your left as you enter the tree-lined entrance driveway you see the practice fairway with the teeing area toward the clubhouse. At Masters Tournament time, you will walk down a gravel path running parallel to the practice fairway; at the end of it you will pass a turnstile manned by more guards, who make certain that you are properly displaying your Masters badge. There are no daily tickets sold to the public for the tournament, by the way—only small badges that entitle the bearer to see every day's action. At Masters time, the clubhouse and the grounds immediately surrounding it remain "out of bounds" to the general public. There are ropes and steel poles surround-

ing the forbidden territory, and many Pinkerton guards see to it that no one enters the clubhouse grounds unless he has permission to do so.

The general public enters the course along a road that passes the clubhouse, professional shop, and locker-room buildings on the left. Since the clubhouse is built on the highest point of land, and the other buildings are on the slope downward to the north, the visitor enters in a slightly down-the-hill position relative to the first tee. The monstrous scoreboard—with every player's name, place of origin, and room for hole-by-hole score for four eighteen-hole rounds—is immediately ahead on the right a little further down hill. To the left, about 100 yards on the level of the clubhouse, is the first tee. From its placement, it is obvious that the first hole heads north or to the visitor's right. Directly ahead of the tee is a long, deep valley, which slopes downward to a point 30 feet below the tee level and then rises rather abruptly to a plateau which is 12 feet higher than the teeing area.

We will call the bottom of the valley, or No. 1 hole, Level —30 (each numeral representing one foot above or below clubhouse level, which we will designate "0" level). It is very important that you understand the variances in the terrain levels, as a great deal of the course strategy is built upon the problems of uphill or downhill play.

Let's go around the first nine, considering the problems of terrain so that you will better understand the golfer's problems in scoring well on the various holes. The prevailing wind is out of the northwest; therefore you should also be aware of the orientation of the holes so as to know where the wind will be helping, where it will be hindering, and where it will cause a cross-wind problem. Let's examine numbers 1, 2, 3, and 4:

Consider No. 1 tee to be level "0." The area at the top of the valley down No. 1 fairway at 260 yards distance is Level "0" + 12 and the No. 1 green is Level "0" + 18. So you understand that the first hole is an uphill hole but with only a moderate upward slope or 6 feet from the tee-shot area to the green. Furthermore, since the hole heads due north, a northwest wind will be from the golfer's left and will be neutralizing the usual draw shot (right to left) into the green.

The second hole is from a tee slightly lower than the first green. The fairway is tree-lined and appears especially narrow from the back tee during the Masters Tournament. The hole heads west by south (240° True) and then dog-legs left to 200° True for the second shot. The tee-shot area is 20 feet below the tee level and the green itself is 75 feet below tee-level. So, the second shot to No. 2 green goes an additional 55 feet downhill.

The third hole starts at level —60. The tee is raised slightly above No. 2 green's level and heads due north for a slight dog-leg to the right. The ground level below the fairway bunker in the center of the fairway is 6 feet higher than the teeing ground level and the green is another 8 feet higher. The result is that the hole plays uphill all the way.

The bunker in the center of the third fairway is approximately 260 yards from the tee. The entire fairway slopes left all the way from the trap area to the green, being 22 feet higher on the right side than on the left. When you add these variations in terrain to the fact of a very small tilted green, higher on the right than the left, it is easy to understand why the hole, although short in distance, is a troublesome one to play.

The fourth Championship Tee is at the same level as the third green. The hole heads northwest over a valley differential (38 to 40 feet) to an elevated green 220 yards away guarded by two large traps on the right and left front of the green. The green itself is quite large but much wider than long, which necessitates proper club selection. A line of trees ends on the right hand side of the fairway before the green is reached and this results in very uncertain knowledge as to the strength of the wind at the green. The golfer is more or less sheltered from the wind by the trees and is therefore often misled into believing that the wind is not so strong at the green. Many shots fall short of the green here for this reason. The green itself slopes strongly from back to front and is very difficult to putt.

The fifth hole, 450 yards long, has a 48-foot rise in elevation from the tee to the green area. It is a most formidable hole. Bunkers guard the left side of the fairway on the shorter line to the green and its considerable length uphill requires a long, straight second shot. Because of the fairway mounds on the right, the dip of ground in front of the green, and the plateau affect of the green, it is a most difficult hole on which to place a second shot close to the flagstick. This hole, according to the designer, Dr. Alister Mackenzie, is of "similar type" to the famous seventeenth or "Road Hole" at St. Andrews, Scotland.

Having completed the fifth hole and being up "high" on the western side of the golf course we now proceed to come back down via the beautiful sixth hole, which plays at 190 yards or so from an elevated tee over the valley below to a devilish green some 30 feet lower in elevation than the tee. There are several very difficult pin positions on this green, especially in the upper left or right hand corners. The tee shot that leaves the player more than 30 feet away from the cup on this hole will result in a three-putt green more often than not. On one occasion, in the 1970 Masters, this writer watched seventeen successive golfers attempting to two-putt to a hole cut on the upper left from positions "down the slope" on the front of the green. Only Billy Casper was able to get down in two strokes and even his second putt was about five feet long.

From the seventh tee, the tee shot is downhill with a second shot to a raised green. The difference in elevation is 8 feet from the teeing area to the valley in front of the green with a rise of 23 feet to the plateau green. Now to the eighth tee and the long climb upward to the hidden 5 par green, 530 yards away. The difference in elevation is 60 feet and sets the course up for the return trip on the ninth hole from the same height (adjacent to the No. 1 green incidentally) back down the steep slope to a plateaued, very small, well-bunkered green 420 yards away. A dangerous situation occurs on the ninth hole should the golfer's tee shot fail to carry all the way down the hill. The golfer is left with a difficult "hanging lie," which requires that his pitch stop quickly on the green's surface—something almost impossible to do.

We have now come back to the "top of the course" for the tenth hole and will immediately start our descent into the southeastern corner of the course for the demanding downhill 470-yard tenth hole. The drive here is almost into "outer space." The player cannot see the eventual landing spot of his tee shot. The total drop in elevation of this hole is 90 feet with about 75 feet of that amount at the tee shot area. The slope of the fairway from high right to low left also complicates the problems of this hole.

The terrain continues to drop lower and lower for the eleventh tee, back in a "cathedral of pine trees," and heads downward to a green 445 yards away. The difference in elevation is 50 feet and again the tee shot area is in a blind spot as far as the golfer is concerned. He tries to stay to the right center of the fairway so as to catch its downward slope and gain valued yardage.

At last, we have reached the "bottom of the course," No. 12. From here on the climb will be predominantly upward on the way back to the high point of the clubhouse area and the eighteenth green.

The twelfth green is 8 feet lower than the twelfth tee, so elevation is not a great problem at this hole. The winds, of course, are for this is a gusty corner under normal conditions. This little hole at 155 yards has cost or won many a championship in the long history of the Masters.

The thirteenth fairway has a right-to-left tilt at the tee-shot landing area. This affects the shot into the green because the golfer frequently must play from a stance with his feet lower than the ball, which tends to cause him to "pull" the ball into the

dangerous Rae's Creek. Of course, the creek itself has a great effect on play at this hole, adding a real as well as psychological barrier to the chance here for a birdie 4.

The fourteenth hole plays at 420 yards, and since the green is 18 feet above the tee-level, it plays to a full 420 yards or more. There is a high spot 8 feet above the tee-level at about the 240-yard mark and then a dip back down into a shallow valley at tee-level again. So, the particularly long driver is apt to face a slightly downhill second shot into the green, a situation that makes the green even harder to hold with a second shot hit with less underspin than usual.

The fifteenth hole is downhill all the way. The green is 30 feet below the tee-level. The area just short of the pond in front of the green is 45 feet below tee-level so that the skillful player who does not "go for the green" with his second shot should attempt to get very close to the edge of the pond so as to leave himself an uphill pitch to the surface of the green.

The sixteenth hole is almost a level hole, there being only a two foot differential between the tee and the green; the green is slightly higher.

The seventeenth hole is not unlike the fourteenth, in that it is uphill from tee to green. However, the tee-shot area on seventeen is 25 feet above the tee-level and the green is another 10 feet higher than that.

The eighteenth green is 70 feet higher than the eighteenth tee-level, but the differential appears to be much greater, because the valley in front of the tee falls away 40 feet. The tee-shot area on No. 18 is 25 feet above the tee, which means it is necessary to play for a flagstick on the green that is 45 feet higher than the tee-shot area. It is easy to understand now why the drive is so important on the eighteenth hole. A long "blind" shot to the eighteenth hole is a frightening one indeed—difficult to judge and even more difficult to execute.

We trust that this exposition of the variances in the terrain at the Augusta National Golf Club will add to your understanding of the difficulties encountered in playing the course. A more careful study of the tenth through the thirteenth holes is suggested. The reader will then fully understand how that stretch of holes came to be called the "Amen Corner."

6
Masters Qualifications

(United States Section)

1. Masters Tournament Champions
   (Lifetime)
2. United States Open Champions
   (Honorary, noncompeting after 5 years)
3. United States Amateur Champions
   (Honorary, noncompeting after 2 years)
4. British Open Champions
   (Honorary, noncompeting after 5 years)
5. British Amateur Champions
   (Honorary, noncompeting after 2 years)
6. P.G.A. Champions
   (Honorary, noncompeting after 5 years)
7. Ryder Cup Team
8. Walker Cup Team or World Amateur Team
9. The first 24 players, including ties in the previous Masters tournament
10. The first 16 players, including ties, in the previous U.S. Open Championship
11. The first eight players, including ties, in the previous P.G.A. Championship
12. The first eight players, not including ties, in the previous U.S. Amateur Championship
13. P.G.A. Co-Sponsored Tour Tournament winners (classified by the Tournament Players Division as one of its major events) from the finish of the previous Masters tournament to the start of the current one

Horton Smith, winner in 1934 and 1936.

7
The Masters of 1934

Horton Smith	70	72	70	72	284
Craig Wood	71	74	69	71	285
Billy Burke	72	71	70	73	286
Paul Runyan	74	71	70	71	286
Ed Dudley	74	69	71	74	288
Willie MacFarlane	74	73	70	74	291
Harold McSpaden	77	74	72	69	292
Al Espinosa	75	70	75	72	292
Jimmy Hines	70	74	74	74	292
MacDonald Smith	74	70	74	74	292

Although Robert T. ("Bobby") Jones had retired from competition in 1930, he reentered the sports world to play in his own $5000 "First Annual Invitation Tournament" at Augusta National Golf Club. Although Jones held the practice record of 65, seven under par, it was thought that his lack of competition for several years might have dulled his edge. There were 72 players in the original field. For this year only, the nines were played in reverse order; that is, what is now the back nine was then the front and the front nine the back nine. Paul Runyan and Jones were quoted at 6 to 1 odds to win while Craig Wood, Horton Smith and Willie McFarlane were at 10 to 1.

At the end of the first day, Jones had fallen behind with a shaky 76 and found himself in a tie for 35th place. Horton Smith, Emmett French,

and Jimmy Hines led the first day of play with 70s while Henry Picard, John Golden, Craig Wood and Walter Hagen had 71s.

Bobby Jones's "magic" did not come back on the second day as he scored a 74 to tie for 28th place at 150. Horton Smith played some erratic golf, eagled No. 17 with a six-foot putt and made three other birdies along with some bogies to finish at 72. The seventeenth hole, now the eighth, played at 500 yards. At the end of the second round the leaders were:

Horton Smith	70–72	142
Ed Dudley	74–69	143
Billy Burke	72–71	143
Jimmy Hines	70–74	144
R. Stonehouse	74–70	144
MacDonald Smith	74–70	144

At the end of the third round, Jones had improved with a 72 but his total of 222 left him far behind Horton Smith, the leader, who scored a fine 70. The gallery was quite unruly as Jones played. Most of the people followed him rather than other stars. At one point, Bobby asked a cameraman to stop operating his movie camera at the short No. 3 (now No. 12) and then Jones put his ball into the pond.

Horton Smith had only two bad shots in his second-round 70, an iron on No. 9 and a bad drive on No. 6. He three-putted two greens but had uncanny shots and accurate pitches.

The third round leaders were:

Horton Smith	142–70	212
Billy Burke	143–70	213
Ed Dudley	143–71	214
Craig Wood	145–69	214
Paul Runyan	145–70	215
Walter Hagen	147–70	217
W. MacFarlane	147–70	217

In the final round Horton Smith was one under par going to the fourteenth green (now No. 5) playing at 440 yards. Near the green with his second, he chipped over a hazard to four feet from the cup and then missed the putt. He then needed even par to beat Craig Wood and a one over par score to tie Wood, who had already finished his round. Smith went over par on the fifteenth (now No. 6) the short hole when he left himself a long downhill putt. From four feet, he missed his second putt to fall behind Wood but then got his par at No. 16 with a good putt when he chipped 10 from the hole. At the seventeenth hole (now No. 8) he again chipped short by ten feet but sank the putt for his necessary birdie.

On No. 18 he hit a tremendous drive and pitched to 25 feet short of the flagstick. His first putt was short by 3½ feet but he made the second successfully to win. It was Horton Smith's first major tournament victory.

Billy Burke had three "hanging" putts in a row on the sixteenth, seventeenth, and eighteenth holes and was the "hard luck loser" when none of them would fall.

Here are Horton Smith's own words describing how he finished the 1934 Masters with a par on the eighteenth hole to win the first tournament:

It might be interesting to tell you my own experience in winning the Masters Tournament in 1934. Craig Wood had gotten an early start, had posted a score of 285, and then had left for the East without waiting to see whether he would win or not. So, early in my round, when I was on the fourth hole, I knew that I needed a par 72 to win by 1 stroke, that is, provided no one else managed to come up with a sensational last round to better Wood's score. At the seventeenth tee I needed one birdie in the last two holes. Fortunately, my third shot on the seventeenth was a short pitch. I hit it to within 12 feet of the hole on a beautifully level spot on the green and quite confidently stroked the ball in for the birdie I so badly needed.

The Augusta National course at that time was played with its present nines reversed, so the eighteenth hole that I needed only to play in par was the present ninth hole, a short 4-par. The hole wasn't presenting too much difficulty, but the wind was blowing hard and the greens were very hard, almost "swept out" by the wind. There was a trap guarding the short left side of the hole, and in trying to play it safe for my 4, I got well over the trap and found my ball about 35 feet above and beyond the cup, with a slick downhill left-to-right putt coming up. Although I knew very well that I should get "up" to the cup so as to leave myself a short right-to-left second putt—a much easier one to hole under the circumstances—I felt that I could borrow quite a bit from the left hill and "drift" the ball down close for an easy second putt. I was both surprised and disappointed in myself when I borrowed too much. The ball stopped above the cup from 3 to 3½ feet away, leaving me a fast downhill putt with a quick left-to-right break—dreaded by even the most skillful putter.

I studied the putt, and at that moment I had one of those "positive" thoughts: Since the green was slippery and the break was fast, all I could do was hit the ball firmly and squarely. I was also aware that even if I didn't hole the putt, I could tie for the title and have at least an even chance to win in a play-off. So I stepped up and knocked the ball right in, to win.

Afterwards, a number of people came up to me and said, "You certainly were confident of that last putt on eighteen, weren't you?" Although I didn't admit it then, I'll say now that it was one of the "longest" putts I ever holed, and I am certain that it was due to my attitude and nothing else. It was the positive thought that paid off.

8
The Masters of 1935

1935

Gene Sarazen	68	71	73	70	282
Play off					144
Craig Wood	69	72	68	73	282
Play off					149
Olin Dutra	70	70	70	74	284
Henry Picard	67	68	76	75	286
Denny Shute	73	71	70	73	287
Lawson Little, Jr.	74	72	70	72	288
Paul Runyan	70	72	75	72	289
Vic Ghezzi	73	71	73	73	290
Jimmy Hines	70	70	77	74	291
Byron Nelson, Jr.	71	74	72	74	291
Bobby Cruickshank	76	70	73	72	291
Joe Turnesa	73	71	74	73	291

Gene Sarazen, 1935 champion.

In beautiful weather, Henry Picard took the early lead on the first day with a sparkling 33–43, 67. Willie Goggin, Ray Mangrum and Gene Sarazen were in at 68, Olin Dutra at 70, Bobby Jones and Horton Smith at 74. Low amateur was Lawson Little with 74.

This year the Augusta National Golf Club's "2nd Annual Invitation Tournament" had a field of 63 players and the two nine-hole layouts were reversed from the play of the year before and played as they now do.

Picard shot a fine 68 on the second day for a 135 two-round total. He led Ray Mangrum and

Gene Sarazen and Craig Wood start their historic playoff.

Gene Sarazen whose 71s brought them in at 139. Amateur Charlie Yates moved into low amateur spot with a 70 for 145.

Craig Wood shot a remarkable 68, four strokes under par, in a blustery rainstorm to move into first place at the end of the third day of play. He had 209, seven under par. Olin Dutra scored his third successive 70 for an aggregate of 210. Henry Picard's game slumped. He started at the height of the rainstorm and scored a 76. There were only three strokes separating Picard, Wood, Dutra, and Sarazen as they entered the last day of play.

With the course rain-soaked and the weather near freezing, Gene Sarazen and Craig Wood tied at 282, six under par as Sarazen scored a rare "double-eagle" 2 on the 485-yard-long Par 5 fifteenth hole, holing out with a fairway wood. Henry Picard shot a final 38–37, 75 to finish fourth behind Olin Dutra who had 74 for a total of 284. Lawson Little, then an amateur, scored a fine 72 for 288 and sixth spot ahead of such stars as Walter Hagen at 293 and Bobby Jones at 297. The first prize was $1500 with $800 to the loser of the thirty-six hole playoff.

Sarazen was actually in front when he got his par 3 at No. 16, where Craig Wood, playing ahead of him, had three-putted but Craig dropped a sixteen-footer for a birdie at No. 18 where Gene got his par 4.

In the playoff, again in freezing weather over

the rain-drenched course, Gene Sarazen beat Craig Wood soundly with 71 against Wood's 75 in the morning round and 73 against his 74 in the afternoon round. From the eleventh hole through the 34th inclusive Sarazen shot 24 consecutive pars. Gene had three birdies and three bogies along with 30 pars. Craig Wood missed several short putts and was in the water twice at the 5 par 13th but still salvaged a 6.

Gene Sarazen's Double-Eagle*

Sarazen turned away from his ball in the wet fairway grass and peered down the long slope to the 15th green, 220 yards away. A freezing wind disturbed the flag and ripped through his protective sweater. Around him, one thousand eyewitnesses huddled together in a crescent that bulged behind the green and thinned out to a single line on either side of the fairway.

Before the green lay a pond. Not much of a pond, really, perhaps forty feet across at its broadest. It protected the green about as well as a moat protects a castle. Yet it was no obstacle on the road to an easy birdie for the player who could put together two excellent wood shots and was willing to gamble.

Gene Sarazen was that gambler. He reached for his favored 4-wood, took another quick glimpse ahead through the mist, and swung away.

He watched his ball as best he could as it sailed up into the haze and over the moat to the 15th green. It dropped on the apron, popped up twice on the turf, and rolled steadily toward the cup as though homing on a magnet. A thousand voices in the gallery screamed as the ball disappeared into the cup for a double-eagle 2.

Gene Sarazen strode down the remaining two hundred yards of fairway between the two lines of shouting fans like a king walking to his throne—the 4-wood held in front of him like a scepter. "I started figuring," said the man who had not cared much for schoolboy arithmetic long ago, "and it was the greatest thrill I have ever had on a golf course. I realized all I needed was par to tie."

Par was exactly what Sarazen got on the final three holes to confirm his tie with Wood, and in effect clinch the tournament.

---

* Quoted with permission from Pages 28 and 29 of *The Masters,* by Tom Flaherty, published by Holt, Rinehart and Winston (1961).

9
The Masters of 1936

1936

Horton Smith	74	71	68	72	285
Harry Cooper	70	69	71	76	286
Gene Sarazen	78	67	72	70	287
Bobby Cruickshank	75	69	74	72	290
Paul Runyan	76	69	70	75	290
Ray Mangrum	76	73	68	76	293
Ed Dudley	75	75	70	73	293
Ky Laffoon	75	70	75	73	293
John Dawson	77	70	70	77	294
Henry Picard	75	72	74	73	294

There were 54 golfers in the 1936 Augusta National "Annual Invitation Tournament." The first round was delayed until Friday because of heavy rains and cold weather.

There were 27 twosomes and the starting times ranged from 11:30 A.M. until 2:15 when Bobby Jones and Gene Sarazen played in the last twosome. The rains had been so heavy that it was feared that boats would be necessary to transport the players around the eleventh and twelfth holes. The bridge at No. 12 was completely under water. The first day of play was in near-freezing weather in biting, blustery wind. The players wore two and three layers of sweaters.

At the end of Friday's play Harry Cooper was in the lead at 70 with Al Espinosa 72, Horton Smith 74, Billy Burke 74, and Dudley, Little, Picard and Laffoon at 75. Bobby Jones had 78.

At the end of the second day, Cooper had scored a 69 for 139 and led Denny Shute and Bobby Cruickshank by five strokes as they had 76–68 and 75–69 respectively. Espinosa, Sarazen, Laffoon and Horton Smith were at 145 to remain in contention.

Again rain forced cancellation of the play and 36 holes were scheduled for Monday. Several of the greens had miniature lakes and rivers on them.

On the final day, Horton Smith gave one of the finest exhibitions ever seen as he edged Harry Cooper out of first place by one shot, 285 to 286. Sarazen closed fast to take third, one stroke behind Cooper. Runyan and Cruickshank were fourth and fifth at 290.

The last rounds were again played in terrible weather. Smith got a break in that he was a late starter and played the last eight holes in calmer weather while Cooper had to battle wind and rain the entire way.

Smith did not get into the lead until the 71st hole. He was three strokes back of Cooper at the morning 18, pulled even at the seventh hole but then fell back twice into two-stroke deficits. He was two strokes behind Cooper with five holes to play but birdied the 68th and 69th holes (No. 14

"Light Horse Harry" Cooper photographs Ed Dudley (left) and Byron Nelson. Wiffy Cox is in the background.

Two famous American and British Amateur champions, Lawson Little and Dick Chapman. Little later turned professional and won the U.S. Open in 1940 at Canterbury, Cleveland, Ohio.

and No. 15 with 3 and 4) to tie Cooper at that point. He went ahead by holing a long putt on No. 17 for a par where Cooper had taken a bogey 5.

Horton hit his second shot 30 feet below the hole on No. 18, putted to 18 inches and sank the putt for a finishing 72 to Cooper's 76 and the victory.

The shadows lengthen as Henry Picard and Horton Smith putt out at the 18th in 1936, the year Horton won his second Masters.

Lawson Little on far left, unidentified player, "Wiffy" Cox and Craig Wood.

10
The Masters of 1937

1937

Byron Nelson	66	72	75	70	283
Ralph Guldahl	69	72	68	76	285
Ed Dudley	70	71	71	74	286
Harry Cooper	73	69	71	74	287
Ky Laffoon	73	70	74	73	290
Jimmy Thomson	71	73	74	73	291
Al Watrous	74	72	71	75	292
Tommy Armour	73	75	73	72	293
Vic Ghezzi	72	72	72	77	293
Jimmy Hines	77	72	68	77	294
Leonard Dodson	71	75	71	77	294

There was a field of 46 players—38 professionals, 7 amateurs and host Robert T. Jones, Jr. in the 1937 "Annual Invitation Tournament." Harry Cooper, Ed Dudley, and Horton Smith were favorites to win. A new name flashed on the horizon of golf when Byron Nelson set a new course record of 66 in the opening day's play:

His card read: 445 343 343 33
              443 444 334 33 66

On the first day Ralph Guldahl with 69 was in second place, three strokes behind as he set a back nine course record of 32 on this card:

              444 344 455 37
              344 443 343 32 69

On Nelson's fine round, he had six one-putt

Byron Nelson, winner in 1937 and 1942.

greens, seven birdies, and one bogey on the short third hole, 350 yards long. Nelson drove the elevated seventh hole 340 yards away, was home in two strokes on two of the 5 pars, Nos. 8 and 15.

But Ralph Guldahl was not to be counted out of it by any means. On the second day he and Nelson had 72s, while Ed Dudley with 69 and Harry Cooper with another 69 quickened the pursuit.

On the third day, Guldahl shot a fine 68 to take the lead away from Nelson who had 75. Dudley shot 71 to move into second place at 212.

On the last day of play, after being all even with Nelson at the turn in lackluster 38s for each player, Guldahl ran into trouble on the last nine. On the short twelfth, he went into the water and ended with a double-bogey 5. Again he hit the water in Rae's creek on No. 13 for another bogey to go three over par on these two holes. Nelson, on the other hand, exploded on the last nine with a course record-tieing 32 against Guldahl's 38 to overtake him and win.

Nelson sank a 25-foot putt for a birdie 2 on No. 12, chipped the ball into the hole for an eagle 3 on No. 13 and picked up six strokes on Guldahl in those two holes. Although Nelson did not get his birdie at No. 15, where Guldahl did get his, another bogey at No. 17 hurt Guldahl's chances to win. Byron finished with five straight pars for his 32, a 70 total giving him 283 to Guldahl's 285. Nelson's card on the last day was:

        454 344 554   38
        342 345 344   38   70

Guldahl's card was:

        454 352 465   38
        345 644 354   38   76

Ed Dudley was third with a final 74 for 286, Harry Cooper fourth at 287, Ky Laffoon was fifth at 290. Charles Yates was low amateur at 301.

11
The Masters of 1938

1938

Henry Picard	71	72	72	70	285
Ralph Guldahl	73	70	73	71	287
Harry Cooper	68	77	71	71	287
Paul Runyan	71	73	74	70	288
Byron Nelson	73	74	70	73	290
Ed Dudley	70	69	77	75	291
Felix Serafin	72	71	78	70	291
Dick Metz	70	77	74	71	292
Jimmy Thomson	74	70	76	72	292
Jimmy Hines	75	71	75	72	293
Vic Ghezzi	75	74	70	74	293
Lawson Little, Jr.	72	75	74	72	293

Rain caused cancellation of the first day's play. Eighteen holes were scheduled for Saturday, 36 for Sunday, and 18 for Monday.

Harry Cooper took the early lead on a 68. Ed Dudley and Dick Metz had 70s while Paul Runyan and Henry Picard were in at 71.

There was a huge crowd of 5,000 spectators at this Masters.

Cooper fell out of the lead with a 77 on the second day as Henry Picard on 71 and 72 and Guldahl on 73 and 70 began to challenge. Ed Dudley had 70 and 69 for 216 so that going into the last round Picard led by one stroke over Cooper, Guldahl, and Dudley, and by two strokes over Byron Nelson.

Robert T. Jones, Jr. shows how he putts with "Calamity Jane." (1938) Onlookers are Byron Nelson, Gene Sarazen and unidentified third player.

Henry Picard, champion in 1938.

Guldahl came closest to catching Henry Picard in the final round. Starting out only one stroke behind he was able to stay that close until he went into the water at No. 12. Ralph was able to pick up a birdie at No. 13 but he was never to catch Picard who finished with a beautifully consistent 70 for 285. This gave him a two-stroke margin over Guldahl who had 71 for 287 and Harry Cooper also at 287 on a final 71. Paul Runyan's last round was a 70 for 288 and Byron Nelson scored a 73 for 290.

Picard won this tournament, it was said, by shooting the last three holes three successive times in 2,3,4, which is birdie, birdie, par. Picard had changed his grip to an interlock from an overlap only three weeks before the tournament. His great consistency was even more remarkable in view of that fact.

Sam Snead putts on the 5th green in the 1938 Masters.

12
The Masters of 1939

1939

Ralph Guldahl	72	68	70	69	279
Sam Snead	70	70	72	68	280
Billy Burke	69	72	71	70	282
Lawson Little, Jr.	72	72	68	70	282
Gene Sarazen	73	66	72	72	283
Craig Wood	72	73	71	68	284
Byron Nelson	71	69	72	75	287
Henry Picard	71	71	76	71	289
Ben Hogan	75	71	72	72	290
Toney Penna	72	75	72	72	291
Ed Dudley	75	75	69	72	291

Billy Burke, who hadn't won a major tournament since 1931 when he was the National Open champion after a marathon playoff with George Von Elm, shot a 69 to take the first day lead over Sam Snead at 70, Byron Nelson, Tommy Armour, and Henry Picard at 71.

In the second round, Gene Sarazen, playing in a stiff breeze that brought rain and hailstones the size of robin's eggs, tied the Byron Nelson record of two years before with a 66. Snead had another 70, Guldahl a fine 68, Nelson a 69. The field was bunched on the leader's heels.

On the last day, Sam Snead had already finished the tournament with 280 when Ralph Guldahl made the turn. Ralph had been beaten out of the last two tournaments but this time would not be

1939 winner, Ralph Guldahl.

denied. He knew he had to score a par 36 on the back nine and went out and produced it. Lawson Little had pulled into a tie with Guldahl at the

Ralph Guldahl on the first tee in 1939.

tenth tee but Guldahl's birdie 3 against Little's 5 at the tenth put Guldahl in front. Ralph made a fine tee shot at No. 12, the hole that had helped to cost him the tournament when Nelson beat him in 1937, but Ralph did not get his birdie.

He saved his par 4 at No. 11 with a good chip. The crucial shot for Guldahl was a sidehill 3-wood to the thirteenth green. He had hit a rather short drive and had a 230-yard carry over Rae's creek. The ball just made the front of the green and rolled to within six inches of the hole for an easy and remarkable eagle 3.

Guldahl needed pars in from No. 13 to win from Snead. He saved par at No. 14 with a good chip from off the green, nearly eagled No. 15, so his bogey at No. 17 did not hurt too much. His 3-iron to the eighteenth green was strong, but he putted to within a foot of the cup and sank the putt for the victory.

13
The Masters of 1940

1940

Jimmy Demaret	67	72	70	71	280
Lloyd Mangrum	64	75	71	74	284
Byron Nelson	69	72	74	70	285
Ed Dudley	73	72	71	71	287
Harry Cooper	69	75	73	70	287
Willie Goggin	71	72	73	71	287
Henry Picard	71	71	71	75	288
Craig Wood	70	75	67	76	288
Sam Snead	71	72	69	76	288
Toney Penna	73	73	72	72	290
Ben Hogan	73	74	69	74	290

This tournament witnessed two sensational record rounds on opening day. First, Jimmy Demaret shot a 30 on the second nine to tie the U.S.G.A. record nine-hole low score set in 1925 by Willie MacFarlane in the U.S. Open at Worcester Country Club in 1925 and later tied by Francis Ouimet in the National Amateur championship against George Voight at Baltimore. Demaret's card read:

```
464 343 454  37
333 444 234  30  67
```

No sooner than the smoke had settled on Demaret's remarkable round when it was eclipsed by an incredible 64 by Lloyd Mangrum. This record would stand until 1965 when Jack Nicklaus would tie it on the way to winning the Masters that year.

At the end of the first day's play, Mangrum and Demaret were in front with their fine scores of 64 and 67, but right behind them were Harry Cooper and Byron Nelson at 69, while Craig Wood and Lawson Little had 70s. Demaret came back with a 72 and Mangrum a 75 to go into the third round two strokes ahead of Nelson, Henry Picard, and amateur Marvin Ward who had scored an excellent 68 after a 74 beginning. Picard's round was unusual in that he four-putted the fourteenth hole. The cups had been put into more inaccessible places after the "easy" scoring of the first day.

Demaret continued playing sound golf. He scored a 70 on his third round to lead Mangrum by one stroke going into the last day of play. Snead had moved up into contention with a 69 for 212, three strokes behind Demaret. Craig Wood had brought in a 67 on his third round to tie Snead at 212.

On the last round, Wood, Snead, and Picard had chances to catch Demaret, but with 38s on the first nine they never got into contention. Demaret finished strongly, having putts for birdies or eagles, all within fifteen feet on the last five holes. He holed one of them for a birdie at No. 15. Just as Jimmy finished, a heavy deluge of rain fell and caught Mangrum with a hole to go, but by then Mangrum's chances were over, as he ended with

Jimmy Demaret, champion in 1940, 1947 and 1950.

Lloyd Mangrum drives from the 10th tee in 1940.

a 74 and second place, four strokes behind Demaret's total of 280.

The New York Times's veteran writer, W. D. Richardson, said that this Masters "was a somewhat drab one because of the ease with which Demaret won it."

Sam Snead took a horrible 8 on the eleventh hole in his final round to slip to 76 and a tie for seventh place. He hit the water on the left of the green, took the penalty shot, dropped a new ball and then pitched back into the water again on the other side. He finally holed out after making the green on his sixth stroke.

Jimmy Demaret's record 30 on the second nine at Augusta National Golf Course happened this way: On No. 10, he placed a 1-iron three feet from the hole for a birdie 3. On No. 11, he sank a 30-foot putt for his second birdie. On No. 12, he went over the green on his tee shot, but chipped back to save his par 3. On No. 13, he was short of Rae's creek with his second shot, pitched to 25 feet from the cup, and holed the putt for his third birdie, a 4. No. 14 he played in normal par for a 4. At No. 15, his second shot almost carried the pond in front of the green. The ball ended up half buried in mud and water. Demaret removed his shoes and had to stand in two feet of water in his attempt to explode out of the trouble. He blasted out successfully and sank the ensuing putt for another birdie, his fourth.

He rolled in another good putt of moderate length on the sixteenth hole, putting him now five under par on the second nine. At the seventeenth hole, his pitch to the green stopped only five feet from the flagstick and with another one-putt, he had his sixth birdie on the back nine. At the eighteenth green, he just missed holing another birdie putt. Demaret putted only twelve times on his way to this remarkable score for nine holes. The record would stand for twenty-seven years, until aging Ben Hogan tied the mark in his third round of the 1967 Masters Tournament.

This is the description of Lloyd Mangrum's course record round of 64 in the 1940 Masters by the *New York Times* reporter W. D. Richardson: "In the course of his round he was never off the fairway nor in bunkers, hit every green in regulation figures (or less) and three-putted on only one green."

His round hole-by-hole:

No. 1, 400 yards, par 4—Drive and No. 5 iron to thirty feet, two putts for a par.

No. 2, 525 yards, par 5—Drive and brassie to within forty feet, two putts for a birdie 4.

No. 3, 350 yards, par 4—Drive and No. 7 iron to six feet, one putt for a birdie 3.

No. 4, 190 yards, par 3—No. 2 iron to thirty-five feet, two putts for a par.

No. 5, 440 yards, par 4—Drive and No. 4 iron to forty feet, two putts for a par.

No. 6, 185 yards, par 3—No. 6 iron to twenty feet, two putts.

The gallery heads up the 8th fairway in 1940.

No. 7, 370 yards, par 4—Drive and No. 9 iron to fifteen feet, two putts.

No. 8, 510 yards, par 5—Drive and spoon to fifteen feet, two putts.

No. 9, 430 yards, par 4—Drive and No. 7 iron to fifteen feet, one putt for a birdie.

No. 10, 470 yards, par 4—Drive and No. 4 wood to twenty-five feet, three putts for a bogey.

No. 11, 415 yards, par 4—Drive and No. 7 iron to twenty feet, two putts for a par.

No. 12, 155 yards, par 3—No. 6 iron to six feet, one putt for a birdie 2.

No. 13, 480 yards, par 5—Drive and No. 4 wood to twenty feet, two putts for a birdie 4.

No. 14, 425 yards, par 4—Drive and No. 7 iron to fifteen feet, two putts for a par.

No. 15, 485 yards, par 5—Drive and brassie to forty feet, two putts for a birdie 4.

No. 16, 145 yards, par 3—No. 7 iron to ten feet, two putts for a par.

No. 17, 400 yards, par 4—Drive and No. 8 iron to twenty-five feet, one putt for a birdie 3.

No. 18, 425 yards, par 4—Drive and No. 7 iron to thirty feet, one putt for a birdie 3.

14
The Masters of 1941

1941

Craig Wood	66	71	71	72	280
Byron Nelson	71	69	73	70	283
Sam Byrd	73	70	68	74	285
Ben Hogan	71	72	75	68	286
Ed Dudley	73	72	75	68	288
Sam Snead	73	75	72	69	289
Vic Ghezzi	77	71	71	70	289
Lawson Little, Jr.	71	70	74	75	290
Lloyd Mangrum	71	72	72	76	291
Harold McSpaden	75	74	72	70	291
Willie Goggin	71	72	72	76	291

Craig Wood, winner in 1941.

The time of Craig Wood, previously "always the bridesmaid," had finally come. A winner of some sixteen tournaments of lesser importance, he had finished second in the U. S. Open, the British Open, and the P.G.A. Championship, either by bowing in the last holes in playoffs or in the final match. Horton Smith had "stolen" the 1934 Masters with his sparkling finish and it took the "miracle shot" of Gene Sarazen on the fifteenth hole in 1935 to force the resulting playoff. True to his golfing luck, Craig lost it.

In the 1941 Masters Wood started out with a beautifully played 66 on the opening day of the 1941 tournament and at nightfall found himself five strokes ahead of the field. Byron Nelson loomed ominously behind him. Nelson had beaten Wood in a playoff for the U. S. Open at Philadelphia in 1939, and might prove to be Craig's nemesis again.

Ed Dudley, one of the great players who never won the Masters. He finished 4th, 3rd, 4th, 5th, 6th and 7th in the stretch from 1934 to 1941.

Craig Wood explodes from the bunker at #18.

Nelson's second round was a 69 and pulled him within three strokes of Wood. Wood, at 71, had saved his second day by one-putting each of the last four holes. On the third day, a surprising challenge came from ex-Yankee outfielder Sam Byrd now turned professional golfer. Sam had a 68 to move himself two strokes past Nelson to second place. Nelson worked hard for a 73 and third place again, five strokes behind Craig Wood.

On the final day, at the end of nine holes the five-stroke lead Craig Wood had started with had all been dissipated. Nelson had shot a great 33 to Wood's 38 and it appeared that Wood was destined to lose once more.

The thirteenth hole was the crucial turning point in the hole-by-hole battle for first place between Wood and Nelson. Wood was playing ahead of Nelson. He reached the 5-par thirteenth safely with his second shot, a wood, barely over Rae's creek but on the edge of the green. He managed to chip well to four feet from the hole and seized the birdie with a true putt.

Nelson played the same hole a few minutes later, went wide to the right with his tee shot, and thus lengthened his distance to the green. Nelson's second, also a wood, fell just short of reaching the green and Rae's creek had extracted its toll from another victim. For Nelson a 6, for Wood a 4 on the thirteenth. Wood gained confidence as the report of Nelson's trouble spread to the fifteenth hole, where Craig was attempting to "nail the door shut." Wood had a birdie 4 at No. fifteen and a birdie 2 at No. sixteen. Craig was home, Masters Champion at last.

15
The Masters of 1942

1942

Byron Nelson	68	67	72	73	280
Play off					69
Ben Hogan	73	70	67	70	280
Play off					70
Paul Runyan	67	73	72	71	283
Sam Byrd	68	68	75	74	285
Horton Smith	67	73	74	73	287
Jimmy Demaret	70	70	75	75	290
E. J. Harrison	74	70	71	77	292
Lawson Little, Jr.	71	74	72	75	292
Sam Snead	78	69	72	73	292
Gene Kunes	74	74	74	71	293
Chick Harbert	73	73	72	75	293

By Masters time in 1942, the United States of America had been at war for four months. The future of the tournament appeared to be dim. When invitations to 88 players were sent out by the Tournament Committee, only 42 were able to respond favorably. The field was the smallest in the nine years of the Tournament's history.

On the first day, Horton Smith flashed some of his old "sweet swinging" form and "magic wand" putting stroke for a 67. Paul Runyan matched that score for a first-day tie. Byron Nelson and Sam Byrd were at 68, Demaret at 70 and little Ben Hogan, who was now winning everything in the money tournaments, but no important titles, scored a 73. Bob Jones had a fine par 72, only the

Byron Nelson and Ben Hogan on the first tee in spring 1942 about to begin their memorable playoff. Final result, Byron 69, Ben 70.

A youthful Byron Nelson allows an official to check
his card in 1942. Note Ben Hogan at lower right.

second time he had been able to score that well in the Masters, his "own" course.

Nelson's second round was a fine one as he closed up the gap on the leaders and started to make his move. He shot a 67, and his two day total of 135 for 36 holes set a new 36-hole record, two strokes under Wood's 137 in the 1941 Masters. Ben Hogan had a 70 for 143 and was eight strokes out of first. Sam Byrd was again making his presence known. He had scored a 68 on the first day and was back on the second day with a 69 to be only one stroke behind Nelson. However, he would eventually shoot himself out of contention, for the second year in a row.

On the third day, Hogan shot a great 67 while Nelson cooled off. The fight for the lead narrowed to just three strokes as the final day started. By the 16th hole of the final round, Ben had picked up one stroke on Byron and now trailed by just two strokes. Hogan parred No. 17, playing ahead of Byron who had bogied. Only one stroke of the lead remained with Nelson. Ben jammed his second shot a mere three feet from the eighteenth hole, and when Nelson could not match Hogan's birdie, suddenly there was a tie and the second playoff in Masters history resulted.

In the playoff, Byron Nelson started off with a shocking 6. His opening drive ran under a small fir tree on the right. He chopped the ball out left-handed, put his third shot over the green, and Ben

The start of a practice round. Left to right, Robert T. Jones, Jr., Ed Dudley, Ben Hogan, Byron Nelson.

Former Yankee star, Sam Byrd, on the first tee.

Famous sports announcer, Bill Stern, congratulates
both Ben Hogan and Byron Nelson on their fine golf
in the 1942 playoff.

Ben Hogan and Byron Nelson on the 2nd green.

had him by two strokes. At the fourth hole, Byron found a bunker and Hogan was three strokes ahead.

The sixth hole saw a swing in the scores. Ben pulled his tee-shot off the green to the left and picked up his first bogey. Nelson planted a gorgeous iron eight feet from the cup, holed the putt for a deuce, and now was only one stroke down. Nelson began to make his comeback, heartened by the change in fortune at the sixth. He almost got a birdie at No. 7 while Hogan scrambled to save his par. Then, as so often has happened in Masters history, the uphill eighth again became a turning point in an historic match. Byron was 510 yards away from the cup as he stood on the tee of the eighth hole. Two beautiful wood shots later he was six feet away from the flagstick. Of course, he got his eagle 3. Ben was getting shaky now, had hooked on his second shot, again scrambled for a par. The lead was gone. Byron led by one stroke through the ninth.

The play of both players was equally as good and most dramatic on the second nine. Nelson gained another stroke on Hogan at No. 10, as Ben missed making his chip and one-putt from the edge of the green. It was Byron for a two-foot birdie 2 at No. 12 as Ben nearly put his tee-shot into the water at greenside. Byron was now three strokes ahead and closing fast.

Both players birdied the thirteenth hole. Ben got a birdie 3 at No. 14 and was then only two strokes down to Byron. Ben followed it up with a birdie over the water on the dangerous fifteenth hole. Byron began to show signs of weakening as he three-putted the huge green for a par 5. Now, only one stroke down to Byron at the sixteenth tee, Ben made a mistake that eventually cost him the title. His tee-shot hit the bunker guarding the green on the right. Byron, shooting last of course, could sense victory within his grasp. He stroked a crisp iron to four feet from the flagstick and, no doubt, breathed a sigh of relief. Ben could not get "up and down" from the bunker, settled for a bogey 4 and went to the 17th tee with a two-stroke deficit staring him in the face.

The seventeenth was parred by both players, Nelson with ease, Hogan with difficulty after a chip and one putt. It was all over apparently when Ben's tee-shot at No. 18 hit a tree on the right hand side of the fairway, fell short and left him a full 3-wood to the hidden flagstick on the plateau green some 220 yards away. Ben almost accomplished the demanding shot, but caught the sand in the front bunker instead. But Byron hit a bunker also and not until both players had recovered to ten feet from the hole was it obvious that Byron would win. Ben sank his 10-footer, requiring Byron merely to two-putt from his ten-foot position to win. Byron Nelson did just that, took his 5 and had won with a comeback 69 to Hogan's 70. A more dramatic playoff in any championship tournament would seldom be seen.

16
The Masters of 1946

1946

Herman Keiser	69	68	71	74	282
Ben Hogan	74	70	69	70	283
Bob Hamilton	75	69	71	72	287
Ky Laffoon	74	73	70	72	289
Jimmy Demaret	75	70	71	73	289
Jim Ferrier	74	72	68	75	289
Sam Snead	74	75	70	71	290
Clayton Heafner	74	69	71	76	290
Byron Nelson	72	73	71	74	290
Chick Harbert	69	75	76	70	290

At last the War was over and the fairways at the Augusta National could be reclaimed from the livestock who had enjoyed its lush pastureland for more than three years. The greens were once more shaved with razor-sharp mowers as 51 players, professionals and amateurs, began the first Masters Tournament in four years. Nelson and Hogan found themselves, as might be expected, favorites to win this Masters. Unknown Herman Keiser was also entered in this event, his invitation coming as a result of being in ninth place among the professional golfers in money earnings that year with the tremendous sum of $3,576 to his credit. At one time Herman had served an apprenticeship under Horton Smith at Hickory Hills in Springfield, Missouri, and somewhere along the way he had picked up Horton's smooth stroke and confident attitude.

Herman Keiser, champion in 1946.

Keiser was an early starter in the 1946 Masters and before one o'clock of the first day, he was in the clubhouse with a fine 69. So was long-hitting Melvin ("Chick") Harbert, another new face for

Lloyd Mangrum with Herman Keiser, Masters Champion in 1946. "The putt that got away."

the Masters fans to watch. Keiser's first round showed 26 putts. On the second day, Herman again putted like a demon and was in with an even better 68 for the second day.

An "unknown" had taken a five-stroke lead in the Masters. And who was second? Jimmy Thomson, only a moderate threat in spite of his booming drives. Where were Ben and Byron? Seven and eight strokes behind Keiser at 145.

At the end of the third day, it was still Keiser by five strokes although Ben Hogan had started to move closer with a 69, which included three birdies out of the last four holes. Herman, incidentally, appeared to be weakening in his third round, but scored a magnificent eagle 3 on the fifteenth hole to help calm his nerves.

On the final day, Keiser's game was extremely shaky, and yet when he had to get the ball into

the hole he was able, much of the time, to do it. Keiser played his round a half hour ahead of Ben Hogan. This was not an enviable position. Knowledge of the scores you had to match is much better than the ominous expectation of what Ben "might" or "probably" would do.

Keiser got only two pars on the first nine, but with three hard-earned birdies cancelled most of the bogies for a 37 start. Ben made the same nine holes in 35 strokes. The margin was now only three strokes.

Keiser managed to par eight straight holes on the second nine, trying desperately to keep a solid lead in front of Ben. Ben, meanwhile, had been able to nail down two beautiful birdies, one at No. 12 on a fifteen-foot putt and a great downhill two-putt for a 4 at No. 13. Two strokes of the three-stroke lead were gone. Now Herman was at No. 18

Herman Keiser, 1946 Masters Champion, in front of the clubhouse.

Ben Hogan and Clayton Heafner leaving the 18th green.

and trying hard to get his four there. His drive ended in the left rough, but from there he played a courageous iron straight to the flagstick. The ball careened off the pole and rolled 25 feet away, beyond the pole, leaving Herman a dangerous downhill sliding putt. Keiser charged for the birdie, missed, and found himself staring at a five foot "comeback putt" to save par. He missed that, too, and settling for a bogey 5, was sure that Ben now could and would catch him in the three holes Hogan had yet to play. All Ben needed to win was one birdie and two pars. But those last three holes are extremely hard holes to birdie, especially when a birdie somewhere on one of them is absolutely required. Ben parred No. 16 and one birdie chance was gone. On No. 17 it appeared that he would make his move, but his putt burned the cup and stayed out. One last chance: birdie the 18th and win. Ben's drive was perfect, his second skidded to a stop only 12 feet from the hole. Just knock this putt in for the first Masters Championship for Ben Hogan. Make up for that Byron Nelson beating of 1942!

Ben surveyed the twelve-footer in his inimitable businesslike style. The cigarette had been thrown away; the white cap set even more purposefully on his head. At last he assumed his stance, rather stiff-legged and immovable. The stroke was not a good one. The slippery green had taken its toll. The ball never came close to the cup, but seemed to gather momentum as it passed, slipped farther and farther on to what was later estimated to be two feet, six inches away from the hole.

Those two and a half feet turned into a nightmare for Ben as he carefully lined up his stance and once more failed to hole the putt. Incredibly, Ben had three-putted from twelve feet to lose the coveted title once more. Herman Keiser, the former "unknown," was the new Masters Champion. Would Ben Hogan ever win?

17
The Masters of 1947

1947

Jimmy Demaret	69	71	70	71	281
Byron Nelson	69	72	72	70	283
Frank Stranahan	73	72	70	68	283
Ben Hogan	75	68	71	70	284
Harold McSpaden	74	69	70	71	284
Henry Picard	73	70	72	71	286
Jim Ferrier	70	71	73	72	286
Ed Oliver, Jr.	70	72	74	71	287
Chandler Harper	77	72	68	70	287
Lloyd Mangrum	76	73	68	70	287
Toney Penna	71	70	75	71	287
Dick Metz	72	72	72	71	287

Jimmy Demaret had won the 1940 Masters by a comfortable four-stroke margin, but he really reached his peak in the year of 1947. He was top moneywinner with $24,000 as purses became more remunerative for the postwar professional golfer. He won the Vardon Cup in 1947, for the lowest scoring average of the year, a mere 69.90 strokes per round.

Demaret either was the leader or co-leader of the 1947 Masters from start to finish, and eventually won by two strokes over perennial Byron Nelson. Surprisingly, an amateur contender, Frank Stranahan, finished with two great rounds of 70 and 68 to tie Nelson for second. Cary Middlecoff, a young dentist and fine amateur player from

Jim Turnesa and Frank Stranahan. Stranahan, an amateur at the time, finished third.

The starting field in 1947 poses at the first tee.

Byron Nelson driving from the first tee.

One of the first large scoreboards. Notice that the
names are not in alphabetical order but were moved
around, each on its own panel.

Memphis, had just turned professional. He made
his presence known in this tournament with a
great 71–69 thirty-six-hole start.

Demaret and Nelson played together the first
day, Nelson having returned to the golfing scene
after a six-month "retirement for good" from golf.
Nelson and Demaret had good 69s for the lead as
seven other players, not including Hogan, were at
70—one stroke off the pace.

Demaret was back with a 71 the second day and
found himself tied with Middlecoff. Nelson was
close behind with a 72, one stroke away. All the
leaders had trouble scoring on the third day, but
only Demaret was able to overcome the "nerves"
everyone was showing. Jimmy drove poorly but
chipped and putted his way to six out of seven
"saves," with one putt on each of the first seven
holes, an incredible showing of getting "up and
down" when it is necessary to do so to keep at par
figures. Middlecoff soared to a 76 as Nelson remained in close contention with another 72 to remain three shots behind Jimmy going into the
final eighteen holes.

Demaret won this tournament like the Champion
he had already proved himself to be. His fourth
straight round under par, a 71, brought him in at

Jimmy Demaret sinks his last putt on his way to victory.

281 strokes, two strokes ahead of arch-rival Byron Nelson, who closed with an eminently satisfactory 70, and Frank Stranahan, who almost made it even closer with his 68.

Jimmy Demaret thus earned his second Masters Championship award to join the illustrious company of the only other double Masters winners thus far, Horton Smith and Byron Nelson.

1948 winner, Claude Harman.

18
The Masters of 1948

1948

Claude Harmon	70	70	69	70	279
Cary Middlecoff	74	71	69	70	284
Chick Harbert	71	70	70	76	287
Jim Ferrier	71	71	75	71	288
Lloyd Mangrum	69	73	75	71	288
Ed Furgol	70	72	73	74	289
Ben Hogan	70	71	77	71	289
Byron Nelson	71	73	72	74	290
Harry Todd	72	67	80	71	290
Herman Keiser	70	72	76	73	291
Bobby Locke	71	71	74	75	291
Dick Metz	71	72	75	73	291

This Masters saw "the day of the Club Professional." Rarely is it possible for a club "teaching pro" to win an Open, a P.G.A. Championship, a Masters. He watches too many bad swings of his club members, does not have the time to play and practice golf the way the touring professionals can, is not under the constant pressure, shot by shot, hole by hole, to produce a low score day after day.

Here in this Masters was Claude Harmon—rather short, stocky, a little rotund about the middle—playing in this great Masters tournament alongside a Hogan, a Nelson, a Snead. How did he ever get on the guest list anyhow? It seems that Claude sneaked in the back door for this tournament. He had played at Augusta National in 1947, but his scores were poor and he finished far down the list. It might have been expected that Claude would never be back again. But he finished exactly twentieth in the U. S. Open in 1947, and as a result received another, almost a "courtesy" invitation, to return again and play along with the "names" of golf.

Claude Harmon did just that. He played along on the first day in a very pleasant 70 strokes. He was not in front of the pack, but in a good position to make a better showing than he had made last year. The eyes of the galleries were watching Lloyd Mangrum shoot a sweet 69, flashing some of his old form once again, and the long hitting rifle shots of Ben Hogan, who was still trying to win his first major championship. Surely this would be Ben's year to come through with his first victory at the Masters.

An unknown, Harry Todd of Dallas, breezed in on the second day with a beautifully played 67. Regrettably, after his moment in the spotlight, he would shoot an awful 80 the next day and his day and tournament would be over. Would Claude Harmon go the same way? Not so far, at least through two rounds. For Claude returned a nice 70 on his second round. That made it two 70s back-to-back, a very respectable start for a teaching professional.

Claude would "blow up" on the third day, everyone felt; and everyone was already feeling sorry for him. But no, it was Hogan who "blew" to a 77, Mangrum to a 75 and of course poor Todd to that 80. Claude kept plugging along, turning in steady pars and then in the tough "corner" stretch rolled in a 3-foot birdie 3 at No. 11, a 6-foot deuce at No. 12, and made a 4-par out of No. 13 by getting on the 5-par green in two and two-putting. Suddenly it began to dawn on the increasing number of people in the galleries who were watching Claude that he might perhaps make it after all. But the last round was still to be played. They would wait and see. In the meantime, long-hitting Melvin ("Chick") Harbert had established himself as a prime contender, the touring pro who might just take over when the pressure got to the club pro. Harbert had already played three solid rounds in 71, 70, and 70 and was lying just two strokes off Harmon's pace.

On the last day, Harmon struggled at first. The galleries were now pulling for him as the underdog. When he bogied No. 4 and went over par for the first time, the heads nodded. "This is it. Claude is through." He managed to par the difficult fifth hole and came to the tough 3-par sixth hole desperately needing a break, not only for his score but for his confidence as well. He got it. The flagstick was on the left side of the green. Claude aimed his 5-iron a bit to the right and gently drew the ball back toward the hole. He left himself six inches from the hole, for what was practically a conceded birdie 2. He tapped the ball in and from there on nothing and nobody could or would catch Claude Harmon. A 12-footer for a 3 at No. 7, a 3-wood to the eighth green and a 6-footer for an eagle 3. The galleries went wild and Claude knew he could make it now. He had gone four under par in three holes, the sixth through the eighth, and now stood three under for the round.

It was not all over however. Claude lost two more strokes along the way on the last nine, but it didn't really matter. He was so far in front that nobody came near him on that day. Cary Middlecoff's last two rounds of 69, 70 (which merely matched Claude's, by the way) still left Cary five strokes behind for second place. Third was Harbert, the one who did the "blowing up" with a final 76 for 287, nine strokes in arrears. The club professionals of America had seen Claude Harmon raise their prestige immeasurably. From then on, they would walk with their heads held a little higher and smile when anyone said "a club pro can't win one of the big ones."

Cary Middlecoff, runner-up (left) and Robert T. Jones, Jr. congratulate Claude Harmon on his winning score of 279 in the 1948 Masters.

19
The Masters of 1949

Sam Snead	73	75	67	67	282
Johnny Bulla	74	73	69	69	285
Lloyd Mangrum	69	74	72	70	285
Johnny Palmer	73	71	70	72	286
Jim Turnesa	73	72	71	70	286
Lew Worsham, Jr.	76	75	70	68	289
Joe Kirkwood, Jr.	73	72	70	75	290
Jimmy Demaret	76	72	73	71	292
Clayton Heafner	71	74	72	75	292
Byron Nelson	75	70	74	73	292

Sam Snead came to the 1949 Masters riding on a "hot streak." He had just won open tournaments at Aiken, South Carolina, and Greensboro, North Carolina. Since Aiken is only 16 miles away from Augusta, Sam was heartened by his performances on the southern fairways so early in the year. The Augusta National conditions would not be much different. After playing in the previous eight Masters Tournaments, Sam was about to lose the "can't miss" designation the galleries had attached to him. And remember, he had blown the U. S. Open twice in past history, once with that horrendous 8 on the last hole at Philadelphia Country Club in 1939 and again when he missed the 30½ inch putt and Lew Worsham did not miss his 29½ incher at St. Louis in 1947. But Sam was putting well this year—at least, he was putting well for Sam Snead.

Sam Snead puts on the first Masters Tournament "Green Coat" after winning the tournament in 1949. It was then that the Masters Champions Club was formed and that all the former Masters Champions were also given their green coats.

Lloyd Mangrum, with his little mustache and "riverboat gambler" strolling walk, got off to a great start. The winds blew and only 6 out of 58 players broke par. Sam Snead took 73 strokes and rested in eighth place after all the opening-day scores were on the big scoreboard.

The winds continued on the second day. Sam could do no better than 75, but Mangrum had also fallen off his brilliant pace to a 74. Herman Keiser showed that his game was still very much "on" as he clicked out a 68 and tied Lloyd Mangrum at 143 strokes for the halfway lead.

The third day started to tell the tale for Snead. His putter, a new one he had been using only a couple of months, was hot and Sam showed the world he could really putt after all.

Down went a birdie 4 at the second, down went a 22-foot putt for a 2 at the short fourth hole. Now an 8-footer for a birdie at No. 5 and to top it off, a curling 14-footer for his fourth birdie of the nine and a 32 beginning.

While Sam did slip to a three-putt at No. 10 he managed to birdie the two 5-pars, Nos. 13 and 15, and waltzed home with a 67, five under par. Now Sam was only one stroke out of first place, just behind Johnny Palmer who had started with 73 and 71 but had tacked on a good 70 for his third round. Mangrum, with 72, was tied with Snead going into the last day's play.

Could Sam Snead win "the big one" with those ghosts of his blow-ups crowding into his imagination? He could. The fourth day Sam again putted like a demon. He got a 20-footer on No. 1, made a "four par" birdie out of No. 2 by getting home on the 535-yard hole with an iron. He parred the third hole but scored once more with a 15-foot birdie deuce at No. 4. One bogey marred his card on the front nine, but he did make another "routine" birdie 4 at No. 8 to go out in 33 strokes.

Sam got a little bit off the par track as he started down into the 10, 11, 12 corner, but by getting a 10-foot deuce at No. 12 he almost offset bogeys at Nos. 10 and 11. With the victory almost in sight and so sweet Sam Snead could savor it, he turned on more heat with great birdies at the two five-pars coming in, Nos. 13 and 15. It did not matter that he got into tree trouble on No. 18. Sam merely

Ed Dudley (left) and Johnny Bulla. Bulla's best finish was in 1949 when he was second to Sam Snead.

drilled a 7-iron to within 18 feet of the hole and dropped that putt as well for the finishing touch on a great round of exactly 67 strokes.

Sam Snead had won his first Masters in nine attempts by three strokes over Mangrum and Johnny Bulla, who had closed from nowhere with two straight 69s to share the second spot.

Sam Snead put on a new coat in front of the massed galleries surrounding the clubhouse. It was a bright green sport jacket with the Augusta National Masters symbol over its top left pocket. This was the first Masters coat to be awarded a winner of this great tournament. A few days later the order had been put out to obtain the sizes and measurements of all the past Masters Champions. Every one of them would shortly receive his new green Masters coat in a belated additional recognition of his standing in international golf scene as a "Master of Golf."

20
The Masters of 1950

1950

Jimmy Demaret	70	72	72	69	283
Jim Ferrier	70	67	73	75	285
Sam Snead	71	74	70	72	287
Ben Hogan	73	68	71	76	288
Byron Nelson	75	70	69	74	288
Lloyd Mangrum	76	74	73	68	291
Clayton Heafner	74	77	69	72	292
Cary Middlecoff	75	76	68	73	292
Lawson Little, Jr.	70	73	75	75	293
Fred Haas, Jr.	74	76	73	71	294
Gene Sarazen	80	70	72	72	294

This was the year that Jimmy Demaret once more showed the golf world what a marvelous competitor he was. He had won his first Masters in 1940 by the large margin of four strokes over Lloyd Mangrum. He had won again seven years later, this time by two strokes over Nelson. Here he was ten years later still spinning off consistently beautiful rounds at the Augusta National Golf Course. Consider his twelve in succession winning scores: 67–72–70–71 in 1940, 69–71–70–71 in 1947, and now in his customary colorful smiling fashion he methodically produced 70–72–72 and 69 in succession to win an unprecedented third Masters. That this record was made over a ten-year period adds weight to the quality of his play in retrospect.

Ben Hogan was back in the field again, following his serious accident of a year ago. His legs were wrapped in rubber stockings and his walking was on constant "pins and needles." He was in great pain. Ben played gamely (he had made a great physical comeback after his accident, had tied for first in the Los Angeles Open in January of 1950), but the strain of the physical exertion took its toll on him after three great beginning rounds of 73, 68 and 71. Ben stumbled in with a final 76 for a 288 total, five strokes behind Demaret.

Ben Hogan on the first tee as Jimmy Demaret waits his turn.

The suspense of this tournament was not that Demaret won the title again, but the fact that Jim Ferrier apparently had the victory in his grasp and then bogeyed his way into the clubhouse to let Demaret have the trophy so undisputedly.

Ferrier had solved the Augusta National's slick greens in his first rounds. On the first day, in a 70, Ferrier took 27 putts. That meant that he was nine under putting par and yet only two under the course's par. A remarkable record of saving par.

On the second day Jim Ferrier sank six birdie putts. This time he had not been forced to "scramble" so much. His score, a 67, showed it.

Demaret lay five strokes back of Ferrier going into the third day. With the pressure mounting, it might have been expected that experienced Demaret would gain on Ferrier in the third round. It wasn't that Ferrier was unexperienced in tournament play; it was just that Demaret, you might say, practically "owned" the Augusta course and psychologically he certainly had an edge over Ferrier as the climactic last rounds came up.

On the third day Ferrier played raggedly, but once more his putter saved him from serious disaster. His score was a 73, but the putt total was just 29. Nor did Jimmy Demaret make much of a move to catch Ferrier either. Demaret, with a 72, gained only one stroke and went into the last day four strokes away.

Incidentally, both Hogan and Sam Snead were making threatening motions at this point. They had brought in a 71 and a 70 to go up on the big scoreboard at 212 strokes and 215 strokes respectively, only two and five strokes away from Ferrier. Demaret lay in between at 214 on his 70, 72, 72 start.

Then Jimmy Demaret made the big move. He played the first nine in a respectable 35, one under par, picked up a birdie as usual at the 5-par thirteenth, which he owned throughout the 1950 Masters. For Jim merely had had birdie-eagle-eagle-birdie on the thirteenth. He was six strokes under par right there. He managed another birdie casually along the way in and with a 69, reported in at the scoring tent back of the 18th green with a 283 total, the highest he had had with a hope of winning.

But it appears that Australian Jim Ferrier scared easily. He was still far out on the course

when he learned that Jimmy Demaret was in with a 283. All that meant was that Ferrier, two under par through the twelfth hole at the time, could "waste" four strokes and still win. From an offensive attitude, Ferrier became defensive and his downfall was not far off.

The possible birdie hole, No. 13, was next for Ferrier. If he could get by it in par or better, he was "home and dried" as far as Demaret was concerned.

However Ferrier's drive on the thirteenth hole was a wicked hook into the Rae's creek. A penalty shot and another shot short in front of the green and Ferrier lay three strokes, shooting his fourth to the wicked green. A chip too strong and two putts later, Ferrier had a bogey six. The rest of the story of Ferrier's long hard battle in is too gruesome to relate. Suffice it to say that he managed one par out of the last six holes.

Did Jimmy Demaret back into this, his third Masters victory? I prefer to think that Jimmy won it with a great game strategy that he would shoot 70–72–72 and a final 69 and expect that score to win no matter what Hogan, Nelson or any unknown, whether Ferrier or someone else, might do.

Lloyd Mangrum observing the "classic form" of George Fazio.

21
The Masters of 1951

1951

Ben Hogan	70	72	70	68	280
Skee Riegel	73	68	70	71	282
Lloyd Mangrum	69	74	70	73	286
Lew Worsham, Jr.	71	71	72	72	286
Dave Douglas	74	69	72	73	288
Lawson Little, Jr.	72	73	72	72	289
Jim Ferrier	74	70	74	72	290
Johnny Bulla	71	72	73	75	291
Byron Nelson	71	73	73	74	291
Sam Snead	69	74	68	80	291

Ben Hogan had tried nine times in thirteen years to win the Masters. Perhaps he would be jinxed the way Snead was with the Open Championship, and would never win no matter how well he played. But at least, Ben would always prepare as perfectly as possible for the tournament. He would hit those hundreds upon hundreds of practice shots, the low ones, the high ones, the soft fades he would need at Augusta in order to set the ball down like a parachute close to that hole, close to the birdies.

Ben had not yet regained his pre-accident strength of body and legs. He never would, in fact; but that indomitable will was just as strong as ever before, perhaps even stronger in the face of adversity. In this Masters, both George Fazio with an opening 68 and "Skee" Riegel with 73–68 held

Ben Hogan, who won the Masters in 1951 and 1953.

the first- and second-day frontrunning spots. But Ben Hogan was in a good place, too, after a 70–72 for 142. Ben was playing well. "The putts might drop tomorrow, they can't all stay out of the cup." Sam Snead, as always, was a threat. He had methodically put together 69 and 74 for 143 and, champion that he is, returned a cozy 68 on the third day. Now Snead and Riegel were tied heading down the stretch. Ben was just one stroke behind. Snead and Riegel could feel Ben's breath on their necks.

The only one who came close to catching Ben Hogan after a 33 first nine on the last day was "Skee" Riegel, who shot a creditable 71 for a 282 total, six under par for the 72 holes.

However, Ben would not be denied this time.

He heard that Sam Snead was in serious trouble. Sam had taken an incredible four over par, "quadruple bogey" 8 on the eleventh, the water hole when he just couldn't keep out of the pond there. With Sam finally dragging himself in with a frightful 80 to crash all the way down from a challenging position to eventual tenth place in the tournament, Ben could afford to play it cool and safe coming home the rest of the way.

Ben did. He played each of the two 5-pars, Nos. 13 and 15, short with his second shot and yet he was able to birdie the first one, and par the second. He played the uphill No. 18 cautiously short and pitched to four feet of the cup, sank the putt, and had a 68 on fourteen pars and four birdies. He had won the Masters at last. Ben couldn't believe it.

22
The Masters of 1952

1952

Sam Snead	70	67	77	72	286
Jack Burke, Jr.	76	67	78	69	290
Al Besselink	70	76	71	74	291
Tommy Bolt	71	71	75	74	291
Jim Ferrier	72	70	77	72	291
Lloyd Mangrum	71	74	75	72	292
Julius Boros	73	73	76	71	293
Fred Hawkins	71	73	78	71	293
Ben Hogan	70	70	74	79	293
Lew Worsham, Jr.	71	75	73	74	293

Sam Snead had finished second to Ralph Guldahl in 1939 in the Masters, and then had seemed to settle into an unsatisfactory "rut" (for Sam, that is) in 1940, 1941, 1942 and the first tournament after World War II, 1946, with scores ranging from 288 to 292, far down the list. In 1947 and 1948, Sam didn't even finish among the ten low scores. But then he crashed through with his first win in 1949, on his splendid 67–67 finishing rounds for 282 and a three-stroke margin over Johnny Bulla.

Now it was three years later, and Sam had again gone through the 287 to 291 "doldrums" down the list in 1950 and 1951. Hogan remained his chief rival and now that Hogan had broken the ice with his win in 1951, Sam had his work cut out for him if he wanted to win this, the 1952 Masters.

Sam Snead, winner in 1949, 1952 and 1954.

Hogan was methodical, as usual, and scored a sound two-under-par 70 on opening day. Sam, much less methodical but more spectacular, mixed

Sam Snead, Masters Champion of 1952 tells the Duke of Windsor "how he did it."

a double bogey on the first hole and a water-logged 6 on the 5-par thirteenth with enough birdies to offset those errors and also had a 70 on the board.

On the second day, Hogan put another 70 back-to-back with his first one and Sam merely birdied five times along the way to a front-running 67 and a 137 halfway total.

On the third day, the winds blew at more than 30 miles an hour. The greens became glassy smooth, the ball took strange bounces and did not want to go in the hole. Sam was disconsolate. He had racked up a disgraceful (not really, under the weather conditions) 77. Ben was thin-lipped as usual, "the mechanical man," and while he was "bad" for Ben Hogan he still was able to gain back the three-stroke deficit from Sam, 74 to 77. The two arch rivals went into the final day with a dream situation for the galleries. Surely, relentless,

machinelike Ben Hogan would beat Sam. Sam would skyrocket again. Hadn't he done it many times before?

Snead was scheduled to play an hour ahead of Hogan. Sam played well for eleven holes and then it appeared that the blowup had come. On the dinky twelfth hole with the pond on its front and right, the mean bunkers around its narrow perimeter, Sam dunked his short iron tee-shot into the water. A ball over his shoulder, penalty stroke, two shooting his third shot for the green, still a delicate pitch over the same pond.

Sam almost put the ball in the water again. This time the grass at the green's edge saved him as it held the ball up, but what a lie! Now faced with his fourth shot to the flagstick, a probable two putt, Snead was staring a 6 or worse in the face. And hadn't he met similar disaster last year at No. 11? Sam did his best with a very difficult shot from an awkward stance with one foot higher than the other. He chipped the ball up onto the green, and it rolled and rolled toward the hole, never hesitated at the cup, just plunked right in for a sweet bogey 4, one of the best bogeys Sam had ever made in his life. Sam regained his composure then, settled down, played in the rest of the nine in sound fashion and hung up a remarkable 72 under great pressure. At 286 he would beat Ben Hogan provided that Ben did not score 71 or better. But word had already crossed the course. Ben was having putting woes. Five times, Ben Hogan three-putted. He had only a single one-putt that day. The roof had fallen in on "the mechanical man." He finished with a 79, seven over par, when he had needed only a par round to tie. Hogan was not unbeatable, at least in this Masters. Sam Snead was. He put on with great pleasure his second green Masters coat. Wouldn't he have loved to get Hogan in a Masters' playoff again?

Robert T. Jones, Jr. congratulating Sam Snead on his second Masters Championship in 1952, as Jack Burke, Jr., runner-up, looks on.

23
The Masters of 1953

1953

Ben Hogan	70	69	66	69	274
Ed Oliver, Jr.	69	73	67	70	279
Lloyd Mangrum	74	68	71	69	282
Bob Hamilton	71	69	70	73	283
Tommy Bolt	71	75	68	71	285
Chick Harbert	68	73	70	74	285
Ted Kroll	71	70	73	72	286
Jack Burke, Jr.	78	69	69	71	287
Al Besselink	69	75	70	74	288
Julius Boros	73	71	75	70	289
Chandler Harper	74	72	69	74	289
Fred Hawkins	75	70	74	70	289

In 1953, Ben Hogan was almost 41 years of age. In many sports, a man of that age would be considered to be well past his prime. Not Ben Hogan, for this was the year in which he would sweep the Masters and the Professional Championships of both Britain and the United States in the same year. He would win the Masters for the second time, bringing him even with his great rival, Sam Snead, another two-time winner, for that distinction. Then with the Masters happily under his arm, he would proceed to win the United States Open at Oakmont in Pennsylvania, as well as the British Open at wickedly tough Carnoustie in Scotland.

For ten months after his unsettling failure in the last round of the 1952 Masters and a loss of the United States Open by five strokes to Julius Boros, Ben stayed away from the grueling daily tournament tour. He went back to his practice regimen of hundreds upon hundreds of balls hit every day: high, low, and exactly in between. At last he felt he had come close to controlling the ball the way he wanted to do it, with a soft final left to right action that caused the golf ball to sit down as if on a pillow with very little run after the green was touched.

Finally, as his fellow competitors were struggling with the Greater Greensboro Open and the Jacksonville Open during the two weeks before Masters time, where was Ben Hogan? At Augusta National Golf Course, you may be sure. He had checked in two whole weeks ahead of time, and had played eleven rounds on the course by the time opening day came around. The fairways and greens were in more magnificent condition than usual. Ben was really training his sights on the Masters this year and he didn't care who knew it. At the end of the 1953 tournament, everyone would be able to see whether he had wasted his time or not. At this point, Ben didn't think so. He thought his game was in "pretty good shape."

There are often a couple of "hot starters" in first rounds of the Masters, and this year the pattern remained true. Both Melvin ("Chick") Harbert and roly-poly Ed ("Porky") Oliver were under par with a 68 and a 69 for starters. Ben was quite comfortable resting in third place with his workmanlike 70.

Hogan moved up one stroke the next day with an even more workmanlike 69 for 139 in two rounds. Oliver went to 73 and 142, three strokes away, and Harbert matched the 73 to lie two strokes away from Ben. But Ben had already taken the lead in this tournament, which he had willed he would win. And win it he continued to do.

The next day, Ben had a mere 66 strokes and from then on the tournament was his. Oliver tried to keep up with Ben and made a gallant try. They were paired together and played a great spectators' match. First one man and then the other would birdie; sometimes they would birdie the same holes. Ben was out in 32, Porky in 34. Ben took three putts on the 5-par thirteenth as Oliver made the green with a 4-iron second and sank a 25-foot putt for an eagle three. Oliver made up some of the lost ground there, but never really did catch Ben. The final scores on the third day were Hogan 66, Oliver 67.

On the last day rain came down during the morning, but since the leaders started later in the day, the only effect on their games was the fortunate one of helping to slow up the glassy greens to a more puttable speed. The players could actually "charge" the cup for a pleasant change.

Ben Hogan coasted home in another 69, his fourth straight sub-par round on this difficult golf course, to win by five full strokes over Ed Oliver and the rest of the field. It must have given Ben a bit of wry satisfaction when he found that Sam Snead had finished at 292. This was fifteen strokes behind Hogan, and not even among the ten top finishers; in fact, Snead was in an ignominious sixteenth spot. Now it was on to Carnoustie and Oakmont for Ben! With that determination and will, to say nothing of that mechanically repeating, grooved swing, how could anyone stop him during 1953?

From left to right, Frank Stranahan, Al Besselink, Julius Boros, Lew Worsham and John Palmer. Who would be the winner in 1953? Besselink and Boros were closest at 288 and 289, 14 strokes behind Ben Hogan's record score of 274.

Ben Hogan obliges the photographers by demonstrating his grip.

24
The Masters of 1954

1954

Sam Snead	74	73	70	72	289
Play off					70
Ben Hogan	72	73	69	75	289
Play off					71
Billy Joe Patton	70	74	75	71	290
E. J. Harrison	70	79	74	68	291
Lloyd Mangrum	71	75	76	69	291
Jerry Barber	74	76	71	71	292
Jack Burke, Jr.	71	77	73	71	292
Bob Rosburg	73	73	76	70	292
Al Besselink	74	74	74	72	294
Cary Middlecoff	73	76	70	75	294

This was the Masters that everyone remembers as the one that Billy Joe Patton "almost" won. There was great excitement among the galleries this year as Patton—a "simon-pure" amateur, a Walker Cup alternate player from Morganton, North Carolina—playing in his first Masters tournament fired a sweet 70 to tie for the opening-day lead with veteran player, but non-Masters winner, E. J. ("Dutch") Harrison.

Patton was a true breath of fresh air on the professional golf scene. Big, brawny, possessing a smooth but gargantuan power swing, Billy Joe became the darling of the galleries instantaneously! He would converse with the spectators, tell them what he was "a gonna do," and commiserate with them when he hit his infrequent bad shots. Patton

was also a prodigious driver, giving no distance to Sam Snead or anybody else who thought he could drive the ball far. Whether the ball went straight was often another matter; but here, too, Billy Joe was not only courageous, but also a first-class gambler. Once in the rough, if he could see an opening a yard wide between two big pines 75 yards away, and if that "hole in the sky" led to the flagstick, Billy Joe just "busted" the ball, blithely, matter-of-factly; and as often as not he did get through that opening.

Although Patton told the reporters he might shoot 80 the second day, he did not. In fact he had a nice 74 and lo, Billy Joe was leading the entire field after 36 holes. Ben Hogan had 72 and 73, Sam Snead 74 and 73, and E. J. Harrison a horrible 79 after his 70 beginning.

Could an amateur win it all for the first time in Masters history? Time would tell. In the meantime, Billy Joe kept on playing and playing pretty darn well. He slipped a little bit to a 75 on his third round and Hogan, in typical third-round Hogan fashion, had turned in a par-breaking 69. Now, the professionals would take over, it was thought, for Patton's 75 left him five big strokes behind Ben Hogan. And no "amateur" was going to spot little Ben five strokes on the last round of the Masters, was he? Furthermore, Hogan had more than Patton on his mind. Sam Snead was back again in an ominous position. A third-round 70 had left Sam at 217, only three strokes behind Ben's 214. Remember, Billy Joe was at 219 now or five strokes off the pace.

Then, if ever in the Masters, the galleries went wild. It might be said that "all hell broke loose" to fit what Billy Joe Patton did for the first eleven holes of the last round of this 1954 Masters. Through the first five holes, Billy Joe matched par. Good enough but not climbing up on Snead and Hogan, by any means.

Then, on the 190-yard sixth hole, knowing he needed a birdie badly, Billy Joe proceeded to knock the ball right into the hole for an ace. Actually it was an "almost" ace that wasn't. Joe Dey, of the U.S.G.A. (now czar of the Professional Golfers Association) had to jiggle the flagstick a bit to release the wedged ball and allow it to drop to the bottom of the hole, where the rules of golf require it to be to count as an "ace." The roar of the galleries, it was said, was heard in Atlanta miles and miles away.

Patton—now two under par and rather encouraged, to say the least, by the turn of events—parred the seventh hole, birdied again at No. 8 with his long-ball ability, and capped the nine with another birdie at the ninth hole. He had shot a 32, had gone past Sam Snead who had shot a 37, and had pulled himself into a tie with Hogan, who would later reach the turn also in 37.

Billy Joe got through the tenth and eleventh safely in par, slipped slightly to a bogey at the twelfth, but then Rae's creek did the amateur in. Billy Joe socked his 4-wood into the water. Groans from the gallery. A rueful smile from Billy Joe, but a smile nevertheless. Patton took a double-bogey 7 on the thirteenth. He did not give up at this bad turn of events, however, but came right back with a birdie 3 at the fourteenth. Then, disaster struck again! He splashed his second shot into the pond in front of the fifteenth hole, got on the green in 4, then two-putted for a bogey 6.

Billy Joe parred in from there but his day was gone, never to come again at the Masters. He finished at 290. If he had been able to par only one and bogey the other of those two 5 pars, the thirteenth and the fifteenth, he still could have beaten the eventual tie of Snead and Hogan at 289. But it was a great day not only for Billy Joe Patton, but for amateur golf all over the world. You still hear one amateur say to another, "remember when Billy Joe Patton almost won the Masters?"

Oh, yes, Sam Snead beat Ben Hogan 70 to 71 in the playoff. The play was good but not so colorful as it would have been if Billy Joe Patton had been there.

Ben Hogan driving from the first tee, Sam Snead waiting. The famous playoff in 1954.

25
The Masters of 1955

1955

Cary Middlecoff	72	65	72	70	279
Ben Hogan	73	68	72	73	286
Sam Snead	72	71	74	70	287
Bob Rosburg	72	72	72	73	289
Mike Souchak	71	74	72	72	289
Julius Boros	71	75	72	71	289
Lloyd Mangrum	74	73	72	72	291
Harvie Ward	77	69	75	71	292
Stan Leonard	77	73	68	74	292
Dick Mayer	78	72	72	71	293
Byron Nelson	72	75	74	72	293
Arnold Palmer	76	76	72	69	293

Here is Cary Middlecoff's own description of the remarkable putt he sank on the thirteenth green in the second round of the 1955 Masters tournament: *

In the second round of the Masters Tournament, I came to the 13th hole five under par. On this famous par-five hole my second shot with a three-wood hit on the green about pin-high and rolled about eighty feet past the cup, way on the back of this long green. As I looked over the tremendously long putt, I could only think how nice it would be to get it close to the hole for an easy birdie and go six under par. There were several slight undulations

---

* From the book *Advanced Golf* by Cary Middlecoff. © 1957 by Prentice-Hall, Inc., Englewood Cliffs, N.J. Reprinted with permission of the publisher.

Cary Middlecoff, champion in 1955.

between my ball and the cup, but otherwise it was a level putt with just a small amount of left break.

I decided that the best way to get the ball close was to try as hard as I could to hole it out. When the ball left my putter, I knew I had hit a good putt, and I watched it roll through the little dips in the happy knowledge that it would probably stop no more than a foot or two away, making for an easy birdie. The ball still had about twenty feet to go when I saw and sensed that it might go in. The gallery sensed the same thing when the ball was about fifteen feet short, and a tentative cheer went up. At five feet short, I could see that the ball was rolling at just the right speed and that it was dead in the middle of the cup. And then "plop," an eagle three.

That was about as big a thrill as I have ever got from golf, and several in the big gallery told me it was one of their biggest golf thrills. It put me seven under par, which was the way I finished the round 65. Bobby Jones, host at this fine tournament, was kind enough to describe that round as the best ever played on that world-famous course. And it certainly helped me win the tournament.

Dr. Cary Middlecoff, a graduate dentist from Memphis, decided in 1947 that instead of making his career in dentistry he would prefer to play golf full-time as a professional. Even though Robert T. Jones, Jr. advised Cary not to make this move, Cary went ahead anyway. And, from the success Cary Middlecoff has had in professional golf over the years, no one dares to say that Cary was wrong in making that choice.

At the 1948 Masters, Cary had a most respectable total of 284, a figure that would have tied or won the first, third, or fifth Masters of the twelve played up until that time. Since then Cary had won the U. S. Open Championship when that tournament was held at Medinah in Chicago in 1949, only two years and two months after he had turned professional. Since 1948, in the succeeding six tournaments at Augusta, however, Cary had only finished in the top ten low scorers of the Masters twice and then not with very prideful scores. In 1950 he had tied for seventh at 292 and in 1954 he had tied for ninth on 294.

So perhaps Cary Middlecoff was due, or even overdue to win the 1955 Masters. This tournament started out with Jack Burke, Jr. shooting the opening day "eye-opening" round, a great 67. Then Burke moved out of the picture to return, as we shall see, the next year in the 1956 Masters with a strong start and a strong finish as well.

Sam Snead opened with what appeared to be the makings of a sensational sub-par round only to take a shocking 8 on the 5-par thirteenth when he repeatedly hacked at a buried ball in the newly installed left bunker there. Snead's 72 "might have been" a 69 easily but for that bad hole. It really didn't matter in the long run however because this tournament was practically over and won by Cary Middlecoff on a marvelous second-round 65. Cary had started with a par 72 and his second-round eighteen-hole score gave him 137 and skyrocketed him at the halfway point into a lead that he never relinquished.

On Cary's great round, his first nine started off rather unremarkably with a birdie at No. 1 and then four straight pars. Then the lightning struck and Cary drilled in one, two, three, four straight birdies to finish the nine at 31, a new course record.

Nos. 10, 11, and 12 fell in comfortable pars to Cary. The wicked thirteenth was next, with its threat of trouble in Rae's Creek. If Cary could just get by here in par, he might get a 67. His drive was a bit too far right. It was long enough, but left a long wood second to the green—if Cary dared to try to carry over the rocky chasm with its rushing torrent of water. The gallery murmured with approbation as they saw Cary pull out a wood, his 3-wood. "He's going for it!"

Considering the trajectory of the wood and that the pin was placed on the very front of the green, it was very unlikely that Cary's ball would stop anywhere near the flag. The shot was struck, a good one, and to the delight of the gallery and no doubt the relief of Cary Middlecoff, the ball just carried to the front edge of the green, but on landing it took off for the rear part of the green and finally rolled to a stop at a distance that has been estimated as between 75 and 85 feet from the flagstick.

Cary would have been pleased merely to take two putts and get another birdie here. He really feared a three-putt green because of the extreme distance between his ball and the hole, to say nothing of the subtle undulations in the monstrous green, one of the largest at Augusta.

Cary surveyed the long putt in his inimitable style. He hitched up his trousers again and again, adjusted the peak of his white-visored cap, and stalked the perimeter of the line to the cup in intense concentration. Cary was a great "house-keeper," too, and no green ever satisfied him until he had found a piece of gravel or cut grass on his line and thrown it away dramatically.

Finally, he crouched well over the ball, head directly above it with his mallet-head putter in front of the ball, then behind it, then possibly once more in front of the ball and behind it again. At last, a slow, beautiful takeaway and the ball was on its way toward the distant cup. Would the putt be long enough? The green was slick and though it appeared at first that the ball might stop short of two-putt distance, it could be seen to be coming closer and closer to the cup. As you know from Cary's own description at the beginning of this chapter, the ball did go in.

Middlecoff's 65 put him four strokes ahead of his nearest challenger, Ben Hogan, who had brought in a fine 68 after a 73 on the first round.

Hogan and Middlecoff matched third-round 72s

and Cary was "in" if he could only keep plugging away at par and force Ben or anyone else to shoot a "miracle" round to catch him. Sam Snead and Bob Rosburg were respectively six and seven strokes behind.

All Cary did on the final day was play the front nine in 34, two under par, and stayed right there in front all the way for a 70 and a total of 279 strokes, a score second only to Ben Hogan's remarkable 274 in 1953. Cary won by a new record margin of seven strokes over the second-place finisher, Hogan, who brought in another badly putted round (for Ben, that is) of 73 strokes.

It is noteworthy that Arnold Palmer made his first appearance in the top ten finishers of the Masters in this tournament, when after a lack-luster start of two 76s he came back with 72 and 69. It would be three more years before the start of the Arnold Palmer "every other year" win of the Masters.

26
The Masters of 1956

1956

Jack Burke, Jr.	72	71	75	71	289
Ken Venturi	66	69	75	80	290
Cary Middlecoff	67	72	75	77	291
Lloyd Mangrum	72	74	72	74	292
Sam Snead	73	76	72	71	292
Jerry Barber	71	72	76	75	294
Doug Ford	70	72	75	77	294
Shelley Mayfield	68	74	80	74	296
Tommy Bolt	68	74	78	76	296
Ben Hogan	69	78	74	75	296

Jack Burke, Jr., winner in 1956.

This was another year in which there was a serious "amateur threat" at the Masters. It wasn't Billy Joe Patton this time, but dark-haired, slighter, Ken Venturi only 24 years old and invited to this year's tournament as "a deserving player not otherwise eligible." Ken was a pupil of Byron Nelson and like his mentor he hit magnificent iron shots. He had first gained recognition as a leading amateur of the country by making the United States Walker Cup team in 1953, had spent some time in the Army, and having come out again played well in enough tournaments to catch the attention of his peers and merit this invitation only rarely extended to an amateur.

Ken started off brilliantly the first day—playing, incidentally, with the colorful Billy Joe Patton who undoubtedly was recalling his own day of glory in 1954. Ken was so accurate with his wood shots that he made sixteen greens in the regulation figures.

He had eight one-putt greens, too, and no bogies to score the lowest round ever shot by an amateur in the Masters, a 66. (The record still stands, by the way, and only once has been seriously challenged, when Charlie Coe in 1959 came in with a score of 67 in the third round.)

Defending champion Cary Middlecoff was close behind Venturi with a 67. Hogan had 69. Scores were low on this calm day on which light rains helped to slow down Augusta National's normally icy greens.

The next day, strong winds blew, sometimes in gusts up to 50 miles an hour. The scores, in general, went up. Hogan took a 78, Middlecoff a 72. Ken played very well again, and by scrambling mightily saved a number of pars with good chipping and accurate putting. The highlight of Venturi's third round was a magnificent chip-shot, his third shot to the par-5 8th hole. He was some 35 yards away from the hole, just off the green, but he had to negotiate two small rises in the green. The shot came off perfectly with a 6-iron, rolled up over the "hills and dales" on the 13th green and dropped right into the cup for a most satisfying eagle 3 for Ken. He continued to hold his game together for the rest of the round and finished with a 69, four strokes ahead of Cary Middlecoff who was in second place at 139.

With scores of 142 were Doug Ford, Shelly Mayfield, and Tommy Bolt. (Mayfield and Bolt would shoot 80 and 78 the next day, Ford a 77 on the last day.) But, almost unnoticed behind the pack at 142, rested Jack Burke, Jr. with solid rounds of 72 and 71. Remember, too, that Jack Burke had always seemed to produce one, or even two mediocre-to-bad rounds in each of his preceding Masters, which cost him enough strokes to hurt his chances of winning. He had had a 76 and a 78 in 1952 and only lost by four strokes to Sam Snead. He had had a 78 in 1953 and finished eighth, and a 77 in 1954, good enough for fifth place. In 1955 he had not finished in the top ten.

Jack Burke's third round was a middle-of-the-road 75; and at the end of the third day he appeared to be fighting to finish somewhere in fourth or fifth place without any chance of overhauling Venturi, now eight strokes in front of him. Nor was it thought that Ken could catch Cary Middlecoff,

who had matched Venturi's third-round 75 and remained where he was when he had started the round—four strokes off the leading pace. Incidentally, Venturi had shown serious signs of blowing up midway through his third round when he took an ugly 40 on the first nine to Cary's fine 35, and had at that time gone one stroke behind Cary Middlecoff with nine holes to play. The situation changed on the back nine as Venturi regained his composure along with his putting touch while Cary lost his. Ken birdied Nos. 13, 14 and 15 in a row, came back in 35 to Cary's struggling 40 and the scene was set, everyone thought, for a showdown between the two on the last day.

It is doubtful that Burke felt that he had a chance to move into first place. He was more relaxed, having not shot so bad a third round as usual. So Jack Burke went out earlier than the leaders, played well and hoped that his final 71, a good score but not truly great, would put him somewhere up on the list for more money than his accustomed eighth or ninth place. The 71 added to his 72–71–75 start brought Burke in at 289 strokes. This meant that Venturi, then just turning the ninth hole, merely would need 41 strokes, or five over par, to tie Burke and 40 strokes or less to win—probably. Probably, because Cary Middlecoff could not be counted out just yet. Middlecoff was playing ahead of Venturi and had shown signs of a monstrous blowup on his own part when he four-putted the fifth hole for a double-bogey 6. Cary had managed to finish his nine at 38, which was of considerable consolation to Venturi when Ken took a similar 38 on his first nine; then too, Ken still had the four-stroke lead over Cary and Burke's 35 on the front nine had only gained for Burke three of the eight strokes he needed to get into a tie with Venturi.

Then, the famous "Amen Corner" started to take its toll on Venturi. He bogied No. 10, one stroke of the lead was gone. He bogied No. 11, two strokes of the lead were gone. Nos. 12, 14, and 15 were similar nightmares. Not double-bogeys, just bogeys, and five strokes were gone. Now Venturi really was in trouble. Middlecoff, ahead of him, was continuing to have his troubles. He had three-putted the seventeenth hole after failing to get on with his second shot. Cary was now headed for more than the 289 score already posted by Jack Burke.

Ken's lead was gone entirely. He now needed straight par in, starting with the sixteenth hole, merely to tie Jack Burke. To the great relief of his huge gallery, all pulling for the obviously struggling, weary young amateur, Ken got his tee-shot onto the three-par sixteenth and got down in two putts. He had broken the string of bogeys. Perhaps he could now get the winning birdie at No. 17 or No. 18.

The flagstick at No. 17 had been placed near the back edge of this dangerous, crowned, plateau-type green. Venturi hit a good drive and went boldly for the pin, hoping to crowd the ball so close to the hole he could not miss the birdie.

The iron shot to the green was too strong, and Ken, in horror, saw it roll down the back slope of the green. He had a difficult, if not impossible, pitch to the pin now just to save his par. He made a great effort, now under tremendous strain, for here was the loss of the tournament right before his eyes. His chip came to rest ten feet away from the cup. Those ten feet seemed to be a hundred. Ken did not get the putt down and went to the eighteenth tee one stroke behind Jack Burke. There was only an outside chance now that he could

birdie the 18th hole, pull himself back into a tie and then force a playoff the next day.

Ken played the eighteenth hole courageously. His drive was long and straight, and his second shot skidded to a stop only 18 feet from the cup. The gallery held its breath, still hoping that Ken Venturi, the amateur who had played so well in this Masters, outfighting the professionals time after time, hole after hole, could sink this last putt, and by tieing Jack Burke might eventually become the first amateur ever to win the Masters.

The 18-foot putt barely missed the cup. Venturi had lost—this time. However Ken turned professional that same year and went on to win ten championships in his first four seasons as a pro. As we shall see, he again came close to winning the Masters from Arnold Palmer in 1960, had the tournament "won," in fact, until Arnie put together two incredible birdies on the last two holes to edge Venturi out of the championship.

Ken Venturi did go on to win a major championship, the 1964 U.S. Open at Congressional Country Club outside Washington, D.C., in a drama-packed finish that saw Venturi conquer his own game in the awful summer heat and haunted by the ghost of that bad finish at the 1956 Masters.

27
The Masters of 1957

1957

Doug Ford	72	73	72	66	283
Sam Snead	72	68	74	72	286
Jimmy Demaret	72	70	75	70	287
Harvie Ward	73	71	71	73	288
Peter Thomson	72	73	73	71	289
Ed Furgol	73	71	72	74	290
Jack Burke, Jr.	71	72	74	74	291
Dow Finsterwald	74	74	73	70	291
Arnold Palmer	73	73	69	76	291
Jay Hebert	74	72	76	70	292

This was the year of one of the most sensational finishes ever seen at the Masters—Doug Ford's "hole-out" from the front bunker of the eighteenth hole for one of the lowest closing rounds ever played at Augusta National, a remarkable 66.

Jack Burke, Jr., defending champion, started off strongly in defense of his title with a 71, one under par, strangely the only sub-par round in a huge field of 102 players. The cups were, as usual, in difficult positions, the winds unsteady and upsetting to all the golfers. Doug Ford was practically unnoticed at 72 and 73 for 145 at the halfway mark.

Sam Snead was once more making threatening gestures and had taken the 36-hole lead with a 72 followed by 68 for 140. Burke was still in contention on 71–72, 143 but would revert to his old habit

1957 winner, Doug Ford.

of "ordinary" golf, two 74s for a finish at 291 and a tie for seventh place.

It was Snead who fell off in his third round with

a 74, including four typically three-putted Snead greens.

After a consistent third-round 72 had left him at 217, three strokes away from Snead's leading score, on the last round Doug Ford came roaring out of the pack with birdies on Nos. 12 and 14 and a particularly brave 245-yard wood over the pond at No. 15 to catch Snead; and when Snead had trouble on the back nine, Doug moved ahead of Snead by one stroke as he came to the eighteenth hole.

Doug needed a par there, and if Snead did not birdie Ford would have a likely chance to win by one stroke over Snead.

Ford's drive at the eighteenth hole was a good one, straight and far (the bunker now in the center of the 18th fairway had not yet been constructed) and right down the middle. The cup was cut quite close to the front part of the green, and in trying too hard to get as near to the hole as possible Ford hooked his second shot at No. 18 into the left front bunker. He had practically buried the ball in the front upslope. Now he was faced with a most difficult shot and the strong possibility of taking a bogey because it would be a miracle if he could stop his shot out of the bunker anywhere near the hole.

Doug smashed into the sand behind the buried ball. The ball rose satisfactorily from the bunker, plopped down 10 feet or so from the hole and then proceeded to run straight into it. Doug had saved his round. In fact, he had turned it into a great 66. Snead did not come close to catching Doug Ford. He finished with a respectable 72 which was six strokes worse than Ford's 66. Ford's winning margin was three strokes, 283 to Snead's 286.

Arnold Palmer, champion in 1958, 1960, 1962 and 1964.

28
The Masters of 1958

1958

Arnold Palmer	70	73	68	73	284
Doug Ford	74	71	70	70	285
Fred Hawkins	71	75	68	71	285
Stan Leonard	72	70	73	71	286
Ken Venturi	68	72	74	72	286
Cary Middlecoff	70	73	69	75	287
Art Wall, Jr.	71	72	70	74	287
Billy Joe Patton	72	69	73	74	288
Claude Harmon	71	76	72	70	289
Jay Hebert	72	73	73	71	289
Billy Maxwell	71	70	72	76	289
Al Mengert	73	71	69	76	289

The year 1958 saw the beginning of the "Era of Arnold Palmer" at the Masters. Not since the days of the flamboyant Walter Hagen had such a charming personality exploded on the golf scene with as much attention and commotion as did Arnold Palmer once he turned professional in 1954, after having won the U.S. Amateur Championship of that year.

Blessed with a burly physique and the arms of a blacksmith, Arnold rifled his straight long drives and equally long accurate irons right at the hole with a daring and audacity that caused the galleries to take him immediately to their hearts. Not ashamed of showing emotion, Arnold would wince in pain as a putt failed to drop, smile broadly when an especially dangerous shot came off successfully,

hitch his trousers up and stride forward with a determined face that said to the world, "no one can stop Arnold Palmer when he's playing golf like this!" And very frequently during "the Palmer era," no one could stop him.

Arnold's first important win occurred in 1955, six months after he started out on the professional trail, when he captured the prestigious Canadian Open of 1955 from a strong field. He had not yet won a major championship since then, although he had gathered together a total of seven tournaments of lesser importance. In the 1956 U.S. Open Championship he had made his best showing to date, finishing seventh, six strokes behind Cary Middlecoff at Oak Hill Country Club in Rochester.

Arnold Palmer was overdue to win a big one and this Masters was the tournament that really started him on his magnificent career in golf.

The Augusta National Golf course played "fast" on opening day of 1958. The weather was great, the winds normal, the greens, as usual, in perfect condition. There were seventeen scores under the par of 72 which shows how "good to the players," the Augusta course can be when it wants to be.

Ken Venturi was the lowest scorer with a fine 68. He had now turned professional and was hoping to win the Masters title he had not won as an amateur. Arnold Palmer was at 70 after sundown of the first day. He had been able to score 4–3–4

101

against par of 5–4–5 on Nos. 13, 14, and 15. His long game was especially good. Arnold was making the five-pars in two strokes with long irons. He was putting for eagles and getting the birdies.

Cary Middlecoff, always a threat, was in at 70 strokes alongside Palmer. Others in the running after the first day were Fred Hawkins, Art Wall, Jr., Claude Harmon, and Billy Maxwell—all at 71. Of these four only Hawkins would eventually threaten to win.

Venturi's second round was a typical Venturi display of good but erratic scoring. After a bad four over par 40 on the first nine, including a hurtful double-bogey at the eighth hole, Ken had flashed back in a 32, birdieing the last three holes. He had "saved" a 72 and was still in the lead at 140.

Arnold Palmer was in with a respectable 73 to lie three strokes behind Ken. Middlecoff had done a 73 as well and remained tied with Palmer. Art Wall was still hanging on with a 72 for another 143 total. Maxwell, on a 70, had crept up to 141 but would come back later with 72–76 to put himself out of the running. Doug Ford had had a 74–71 start and was rather unnoticed for the moment at 145. He would make a strong move during the next two days.

Venturi fell off to a 74 on his third round and lost his leadership, never to regain it. Sam Snead had sneaked up with a great 68 for a 211 total. But tomorrow Snead would balloon to a terrible 79 and put himself right out of the tournament. Arnold Palmer was making his move. He had cracked out a 68, too, and now was in the lead going into the last day.

A drenching rain fell during the night. The course was soaked by morning, but it was playable. The skies were cloudy. The tournament officials decided to permit the players to lift, clean, and drop any ball that became embedded in its own divot mark "through the green"—which means all the areas of the golf course except in the hazards. This became a very important decision as far as Arnold Palmer was concerned, as we shall see.

Venturi and Palmer were paired together on the final day. Since they had heard that Snead had double-bogied the first hole with a 6 and was struggling thereafter to his eventual 79, it was clear to the two players involved—and the galleries as well—that the possible winner might be found in the Venturi–Palmer twosome.

Venturi gained one stroke on Arnold through the ninth hole with a 35 to Palmer's 36, and when Arnold went over par again at No. 10 with a 5, Venturi was only one stroke behind. At the twelfth hole, Palmer's ball embedded itself in a bank above the left-hand bunker. Arnold hacked the ball out with difficulty and eventually scored what appeared to be a 5 on the hole. In the meantime, Venturi had made a conventional 3. To all appearances Ken had taken the lead away from Palmer. Then, Palmer remembered the possibility of relief from his bad lie under the "embedded ball" rule in effect for the day. He decided to confer with a rules committeeman (there are rules interpreters readily available all the time at the Masters or other similar tournaments operating under U.S.G.A. rules). Arnold got permission from the committeeman to get relief, so subsequently he played a provisional ball, which he dropped—in accordance with the rules—away from the embedded spot. Arnold made a 3 with the provisional ball and had to wait for a final ruling from the Rules Committee as to which score was his official one for the hole, the 5 or the 3.

Even with this cloud on his mind, Arnold was able to concentrate on the task at hand: to make up those strokes, if they were lost irrevocably. He played a typical Arnold Palmer 3-wood to the thirteenth green on his second shot. The ball came to rest only 18 feet from the hole. Venturi had decided to play the hole safe, short of the green, and chip for his birdie.

Palmer then sank his putt for an eagle 3 to the screams of his tremendous gallery, now sensing a Palmer win. Venturi got his birdie too, with a courageous pitch and one putt. Then came unofficial word that Palmer's 3 on the twelfth hole was to be counted. More pandemonium. Was Arnold truly in front now? Whether he was or not, he was "charging"!

A three putt at No. 14 and Venturi had lost another stroke. He was showing signs of being rattled by the uncertainty of Palmer's score. Venturi three-putted again at No. 15 as the word at last came: Palmer had officially been given the 3.

Venturi three-putted the 16th green and lost his

last opportunity to overhaul Arnold Palmer. The "psychological warfare" was trying on both players as Arnold, too, stumbled in with a bogey on Nos. 16 and 18. At least Arnold was in the clubhouse with a final 73 and a 284 total.

Now there appeared a threat from two late players getting hot in their last round, Doug Ford and Fred Hawkins. If either one of them could birdie the last hole, there would be a tie for first place and a playoff the next day.

Each man played the eighteenth hole very well. Ford got his second shot within 12 feet of his birdie, Hawkins within 16 feet. Palmer watched most anxiously as each man made his last effort to force a tie. It was not to be. Neither putt dropped. Doug Ford would not be a double winner, nor would Fred Hawkins ever again be so close to a win at the Masters.

America had a brilliant new Masters Champion in Arnold Palmer. The "era of Arnold Palmer" was just beginning with this, his first major championship.

29
The Masters of 1959

1959

Art Wall, Jr.	73	74	71	66	284
Cary Middlecoff	74	71	68	72	285
Arnold Palmer	71	70	71	74	286
Dick Mayer	73	75	71	68	287
Stan Leonard	69	74	69	75	287
Charles R. Coe	74	74	67	73	288
Fred Hawkins	77	71	68	73	289
Julius Boros	75	69	74	72	290
Jay Hebert	72	73	72	73	290
Gene Littler	72	75	72	71	290
Billy Maxwell	73	71	72	74	290
Billy Joe Patton	75	70	71	74	290
Gary Player	73	75	71	71	290

1959 winner, Art Wall, Jr.

From 1934 through this year of 1959 there appeared to be a "jinx" on all former Masters Champions. No champion in all those years had ever been able to come back to Augusta and win the title two years in a row. Not until 1966, when Jack Nicklaus at last put an end to this "hoodoo," would there be two Masters tournament victories in a row.

Arnold Palmer took complete charge of the field in the 1959 Masters in the early play of the tournament, although relatively unknown Stan Leonard had opened with an excellent 69 and was only two strokes ahead of Palmer, who was alone at 71. Scores on opening day were unusually high, with only Gene Littler and Jay Hebert registering par 72s to go on the scoreboard behind Leonard and Palmer. Art Wall, Jr. was rather unnoticed at 73 and was tied with Gary Player at that figure. If there were any fireworks coming, Player might be expected to supply them, it was thought. Gary never did, however.

Arnold Palmer returned a well-played 70 on the second day and took over the lead at that point. Leonard had slipped rather badly to a 74 but was able to get fired up again and score a great 69 on his third round and by the fifth hole was tied with Palmer. Art Wall in the meantime was playing along most steadily, putting extremely well on the fast greens. He was in with a fine 71 but at 218 strokes was believed to be much too far off the pace Palmer and Leonard were setting with their 212s. If indeed anyone were able to pick up six strokes on Masters Champion Arnold Palmer in one round, surely it would not be slight, colorless, methodical Art Wall. Doubtless, Arnold would break the "two win jinx" and charge in with the victory.

But in that final round, Arnold Palmer suddenly found himself in serious trouble. Wall was playing in a group five holes behind the Palmer two-some when the news came that Arnold had taken a 6 on the short twelfth water hole. Three strokes of the lead were gone in a flash. Wall had some hope yet. Palmer had put a ball into the water, taken a penalty shot, and then gone over the green on his third shot. He had an unbelievable six strokes on a par three hole.

The galleries were shocked. Palmer had been even par through the eleventh and was showing no signs of weakening now that he was three over par. He fought back to one over par with great birdie 4s on Nos. 13 and 15. He was able to par Nos. 14 and 16. Perhaps he could win yet—get another birdie, and put the championship on ice. But at No. 17, faced with a two footer for his par, Arnold missed. Now he was two over par for the round heading for No. 18. Even a par there would earn Palmer a 74, a total of 286, and force Art Wall to shoot a most difficult four under par 68 merely to tie Arnold. Wall had never broken 70 in a Masters before and with all the pressure of the last holes on him now, he could scarcely be expected to do so now.

When Arnold bogied the seventeenth hole, Art Wall was not too far away to hear the groans of disappointment from the gallery there and get the news quickly via the huge scoreboards when the green "2" (two over par) went up after Palmer's name.

Wall knew what he must do: get some birdies and get them fast, because time and holes were running out on him.

He went after the birdie at No. 13 with a vengeance. His wood second got over Rae's Creek safely but his ball stopped a long 75 feet away from the hole. Art chipped weakly to about 15 feet from the cup. He couldn't afford to lose this "cinch" birdie hole to par. Gently, firmly, Art Wall stroked that 15-foot putt in for the birdie 4. At the next hole, Art Wall, now gaining more and more confidence, canned a 20-foot birdie putt. On No. 15, Wall played boldly, going for the green in two. His shot carried to the putting surface successfully and now he had a chance for an eagle from 25 feet. He did not get the putt down but he cashed his third birdie in a row. He now needed at least one more birdie to beat Palmer's score. Pars in from Nos. 16 through 18 would tie him with Arnold.

The sixteenth fell to him in par. On the 4-par 17th, Art Wall was able to get his second shot within 15 feet of the hole. Down went the putt for his fourth birdie in twelve holes. Now if he could just par at No. 18, he would beat Palmer by a stroke.

Wall hit a marvelous tee shot, a drive he said later was the best one he had hit during the entire tournament. The flagstick was tucked, as it is customarily on the last day, away down in front of the green, daring the player to get close to the hole.

Wall's 9-iron shot was a sweet one, which left him 12 feet below the hole. He would be putting uphill at the hole, a desirable situation on the icy Augusta greens.

With the galleries massed around the eighteenth hole in hushed silence, Art Wall sank that last putt for his fifth birdie in six holes. He had outscored Arnold Palmer 284 to 286. Art Wall's 66 to Arnold Palmer's 74 had gained eight strokes in one round on last year's champion. The "jinx" apparently was still in effect. Jack Nicklaus was coming along soon and he would see what he could do about it.

30
The Masters of 1960

1960

Arnold Palmer	67	73	72	70	282
Ken Venturi	73	69	71	70	283
Dow Finsterwald	71	70	72	71	284
Billy Casper, Jr.	71	71	71	74	287
Julius Boros	72	71	70	75	288
Gary Player	72	71	72	74	289
Wally Burkemo	72	69	75	73	289
Ben Hogan	73	68	72	76	289
Lionel Hebert	74	70	73	73	290
Stan Leonard	72	72	72	74	290

Arnold Palmer came to the 1960 Masters riding on a hot streak. He had previously won the Desert Classic in Palm Springs, the Texas Open, the Baton Rouge Open, and the Pensacola Open. He had not forgotten his weak finish in the 1959 Masters and most purposefully had decided to make up for that lapse by even better play this year. He came to Augusta early in order to get in as much practice as possible. The weather turned sour, however, and cold rain closed the golf course for some of the practice days. Besides, Arnold caught an influenza "bug" and was feeling miserable. All in all, things were not very auspicious for Arnold as he began his quest for his second Masters title.

The defending champion, Art Wall, Jr., was forced to withdraw from the event because of illness, so for the first time in Master's history there was no defending champion on the course.

There were seventeen amateurs playing this year, an unusually large contingent. Among them were Jack Nicklaus, the U.S. Amateur Champion and Deane Beman, the American-born British Amateur Champion. Ben Hogan was there seeking his third championship, but he finished seven strokes away from first place.

With the course heavy from the intermittent rains, the long hitters of golf had a distinct advantage over the less powerful players. In his opening round, Arnold Palmer, customarily a long and straight driver, showed how he could capitalize on his length when he scored three birdies and an eagle on the four par-5 holes. His round was a most satisfactory 67.

Ken Venturi, again trying to quiet the ghosts of his bad rounds at Augusta, was away with a great 31 on the first nine but then fell off on the last nine with a sorry 42 for a finishing 73 and much personal disappointment on his part. He would keep on plugging gamefully, however, and before he finished the tournament, Arnold Palmer would be aware of his considerable threat.

While Arnold Palmer had sprung out in front with his 69, there were four good players right behind him at 71, Dow Finsterwald, Fred Hawkins, Jay Hebert and Claude Harmon. Only Dow Finsterwald would maintain his threat until the last hole.

On the second day of play, Arnold Palmer started struggling. He bogeyed three of the first eight holes and then recovered somewhat the rest of the way, getting two birdies to come in with a shaky 73 and a 140 total at the halfway mark.

Dow Finsterwald came back with a 70 after the 71 on his first round and was just one stroke off the lead. Dow had had the misfortune of a "mental lapse" while playing the day before. He had put down a ball on the fifth hole to "try another putt" as one might do in a practice round once in a while. As he was strictly forbidden to do this by the rules, Dow had to take a two-stroke penalty on the hole. He would have had 69 on the round but for this unfortunate error in judgment. Sportsman that Dow is, though, he had called the attention of the Rules Committee to the fact of the practice stroke. This stroke differential eventually was the difference between a winning total score of 282 and Dow's final 284, so in retrospect it might be said that this was the Masters Dow Finsterwald "lost." On the other hand, it is hard to re-create emotions and physical conditions, and who can say that Dow would have been able to finish his last two rounds of the Masters with 72 and 71, knowing that Arnold Palmer was breathing down his back?

On the third day, Palmer three-putted once and another time failed to hole a four-footer after a fine approach had left him "stoney." His long game was superlative, however, and Arnold checked in with an even-par 72 to remain the leader at the 54-hole mark with 212 strokes. Now there were five men only a stroke away going into the customarily dramatic final 18 holes. Venturi was still in there after a good third-round 71. Finsterwald was, too on a solid 72. The others were Billy Casper, Julius Boros, and Ben Hogan, who would put themselves out of the running on the last day with undistinguished scores of 74, 75 and 76, respectively.

On the last day, although Palmer birdied the first hole as if he were going to catch on fire, he cooled off at the short uphill third hole by three-putting. Then he bogeyed the next hole to the dismay of his "army" of followers. In the meantime, Venturi and Finsterwald were playing a good hour ahead of Arnold so their scores were going up on the ubiquitous scoreboards well ahead of Arnold's.

They were doing very well, too. Each man had nothing but pars or birdies on the first nine and that sight is impressive to see on the monstrous lines behind the players' names on the boards. Venturi had managed to birdie three of the first six holes and Dow had birdied Nos. 8 and 9. Venturi out in 33, Finsterwald, 34. So when Palmer bogeyed the fourth hole he relinquished the lead to Venturi.

Venturi and Finsterwald had a nip and tuck battle of their own going down the last nine. Venturi picked up a bogey 5 on the eleventh hole and the two men were tied at that point. Dow lost a stroke at No. 12, Venturi did not. Dow birdied No. 14, Venturi did not. So the battle between these two fine players came down to the eighteenth hole. At the eighteenth, Dow Finsterwald's second shot to the green caught the right bunker. Dow did not get "up and down" out of the sand although he made a gallant try with a shot that stopped only eight feet from the hole. He had finished at 71 for a 284 total.

Venturi had carried to the green on his second shot on No. 18. By successfully two-putting under pressure-packed conditions, Ken was in with a par 4 for his 70, and a total of 283. He could only hope that this score would hold up before the onslaught of Arnold Palmer, now beginning his last nine.

Remember that Palmer had started out this last day at 212 or four strokes under par for the tournament. Now, as Arnold could see on the scoreboard, Venturi was in with a 70, five under par for the 72 holes. Palmer knew that he must get at least one birdie and the rest pars to tie Venturi, or two birdies and the rest pars to win.

Palmer headed down into the lower corner, parred the tenth hole and the eleventh hole. Then he got by the troublesome twelfth hole with another par. No birdies yet, but the possible "birdie hole," the thirteenth, was coming up next. Surely with his long-ball driving ability this would be a drive, an iron and a two-putt for Arnie. But it was not. The drive was not quite so long as usual, the second was a little wild; so a chip and two putts later Arnold was glad to settle for his par 5. Time was starting to run out. The fourteenth hole is not an easy hole for anyone to birdie, even Arnold Palmer. It lived up to its reputation. Palmer's second shot was a long distance from the hole. Arnold breathed a sigh of relief when he sank his second putt for the par 4.

Now, with four holes to play it appeared that Palmer might be fighting not merely to win but even to pull into a tie with Venturi. The big red "5 under par" on the scoreboard near the fifteenth tee told Arnold more than he wanted to know. He must birdie the fifteenth.

Arnold's drive was erratic. The pressure was certainly showing now. Trying to "crank up" a little more distance Palmer had hooked into the left rough. Here he had trees on the left to dodge and the pond to be carried in front of the green. He would go for the green boldly as ever. The shot went to the right and landed in the gallery, safely over the water but still a long way from a birdie opportunity.

He chipped weakly, missed a 15-foot putt and marked down another par. Three holes to go.

On No. 16, Arnold had had good luck when his chip shot to the hole struck the flagstick and bounced away a short distance. With a little more luck he might perhaps have holed the shot. He got his par 3 but it now appeared that even Fortune was against him on this fateful day.

Desperately needing a birdie on either of the last two holes, Palmer was overly cautious on his second shot to the plateaued seventeenth green. He left himself a 35-foot putt. I'm sure that even Arnold Palmer sensed that he would have to get his tying birdie at No. 18. He could not hope to hole this slippery 35-footer.

At last, Billy Casper, his playing partner, had putted out. It was Palmer's turn to putt. "Do or die." The familiar tensed pigeon-toed stance, the left forefinger down the outside of the putter grip, the steady head, the smooth unhurried backswing. The ball was on its way toward the hole, curving a foot or so from left to right. On and on it came dead on line. Could it go in? Would it go in? Would it burn the hole and spin away? In! Right in the center of the cup, out of sight! A leap for joy out of Palmer as his white visor came off. Still alive. "Now get that birdie at the eighteenth and you can win! At least you know Venturi is tied right now and even if it ends in a tie, you can beat him tomorrow in a playoff!"

Arnold Palmer crushed his drive on the eighteenth hole 300 yards right down the center of the fairway. Ken Venturi was in the tournament headquarters watching the scene on television. Would this Masters be taken away from him in the same way the others were? A birdie on No. 18 is difficult for anyone. A bogey is possible. The monstrous gallery lining both sides of the eighteenth fairway and forty deep around the green itself could almost sense that Arnold would do the impossible: birdie this last hole and win the title outright from Venturi and the field.

Arnie's second shot was a magnificent 6-iron to within 6 feet of the hole. The putt was a little "side-hiller," right to left about three or four inches but decidedly makeable. It was also missable, even by Arnold Palmer (or Ben Hogan, recalling 1946).

Once more the familiar crouch over the ball, the knees locked, the smooth stroke and in went the ball for the birdie 3 and victory. Venturi was shut out once more in what must have been a most bitter disappointment. However, Ken's day of triumph was to come; he would win the U.S. Open at the Congressional Country Club in 1964.

31
The Masters of 1961

1961

Gary Player	69	68	69	74	280
Charles R. Coe	72	71	69	69	281
Arnold Palmer	68	69	73	71	281
Tommy Bolt	72	71	74	68	285
Don January	74	68	72	71	285
Paul Harney	71	73	68	74	286
Jack Burke Jr.	76	70	68	73	287
Billy Casper, Jr.	72	77	69	69	287
Bill Collins	74	72	67	74	287
Jack Nicklaus	70	75	70	72	287

Arnold Palmer was the favorite as he entered this Masters Tournament, but Gary Player of South Africa was the "dark horse," coming into the tournament with an average of 69.2 strokes in his last 49 official rounds.

There was a field of 88 players in this Masters. Intermittent rain plagued the players and the gallery of 15,000 spectators all through the day. Player was delighted that he had lengthened his wood shots and was able to reach the par 5s in two strokes. He scored an excellent 69 on the opening day. Palmer and Nicklaus played in a driving rain, with Palmer scoring a 68, Nicklaus a 70. Bob Rosburg holed a pitch shot at the fifth hole and a 100-foot putt at the fourteenth on the way to a 68, to become a first-day co-leader with Arnold Palmer. Incidentally, Jack Nicklaus was playing in this tournament as an invited amateur for the second time. He had first qualified in 1960 as a result of having won the National Amateur Championship

Gary Player, winner in 1961.

at Broadmoor Golf Club in Colorado Springs in the summer of 1959.

On the second day, Player played brilliantly as did Arnold Palmer, and they shared the lead with almost identical scores of 69–68 and 68–69. Rosburg fell off to a 73, four strokes away in third place. Jack Nicklaus was far off the pace with a 75 for 145, eight strokes behind the leaders.

Gary Player apparently broke the tournament open with his magnificent 69 for a third-round aggregate of 206, only one stroke over the record score for a 54-hole total. The weather was clear and cool as the crowd swelled to 35,000 people. Palmer started his round a half-hour ahead of Gary and promptly birdied the first two holes. But Gary was able to do the same thing a few minutes later. Palmer lost a stroke to Rae's Creek at the thirteenth hole, three-putted another green and was bunkered at two others. Jack Nicklaus came back somewhat with a 70 for a 215 total, nine strokes behind the leader Gary Player.

The final round of this tournament became an anticlimax when heavy rains washed out the day's play after Arnold Palmer and Gary Player had completed nine holes and eleven holes respectively. Player at that point had lost two strokes of his four stroke lead. The eleventh, fifteenth, and sixteenth greens were virtually flooded by the rains, and there was a threat of a tornado which fortunately did not materialize.

Gary Player thought he had "given the championship away" to Arnold Palmer when he staggered in with an unsteady 40 strokes on the second nine to finish the tournament with a 280 total. Arnold Palmer was still out on the course and apparently making one of his famous "come from behind" runs at the leader. Gary had had a ball in Rae's Creek for a double-bogey 7 there and missed a short "nasty little putt" at the fifteenth to bogey that hole.

Player was in the clubhouse as Palmer came to the eighteenth hole needing only a par to win, a bogey to tie. He had picked up five strokes on Gary and put himself into the lead. But the impossible happened. Arnold sent his second shot* at the eighteenth into the right-hand bunker. He had an uncomfortable downhill partly buried lie and now needing only to splash the ball out for a win or tie, skimmed the ball right over the green and down the steep bank on the left hand side of the green. The gallery gasped in amazement. Arnold could still save a tie with a delicate run-up and a putt. But, electing to putt the ball up the slope, he ran the ball fifteen to twenty feet past the hole. He missed the attempt to tie and Gary Player had won his first Masters in five tries.

---

* Later on, in an interview, Arnold was quoted as saying, concerning his bad shot to the eighteenth green, "Before I hit that shot I remember standing there thinking that all I needed to win was a 4, just get it up there on the green and then down in two putts. That's where I made my mistake. thinking about something besides the ball. If I'd just kept my mind on swinging the club properly there wouldn't have been any problem." — *Sports Illustrated*, April 2, 1962.

32
The Masters of 1962

1962

Arnold Palmer	70	66	69	75	280
Play off					68
Gary Player	67	71	71	71	280
Play off					71
Dow Finsterwald	74	68	65	73	280
Play off					77
Gene Littler	71	68	71	72	282
Mike Souchak	70	72	74	71	287
Jimmy Demaret	73	73	71	70	287
Jerry Barber	72	72	69	74	287
Billy Maxwell	71	73	72	71	287
Ken Venturi	75	70	71	72	288
Charles R. Coe	72	74	71	71	288

Arnold Palmer won his third Masters Championship in five years and thus continued his amazing record of winning the tournament every other year. By beating Gary Player in an 18-hole playoff after Palmer had tied at 280 strokes with Gary and Dow Finsterwald at that figure, Arnold also gained some satisfaction for "backing out" of the 1961 Masters and allowing Gary to win that tournament when Arnold took his infamous 6 on the eighteenth hole.

Palmer started out on the first day shakily. He was two over par through eleven holes, then birdied four of the last seven for a 70. His galleries thought that with this birdie streak he would walk away with this Masters. After a 70–66 beginning he was at 136 strokes and possessed a two-stroke lead over Gary Player, who had started strongly with a 67 but returned with a 71 on his second round. Dow Finsterwald was six strokes back when he recovered from a 74 start with a great 68 second round. At the end of the third day of play, Arnold remained in the lead by two strokes after a steady 69, which gave him a 205 three-day total. Player had scored a respectable 71 and yet lost two strokes to Arnold and was then four strokes behind the leader going into the last day of play. In the meantime, Dow Finsterwald with a great 65 had scored the best 18-hole total the Augusta National had seen in seven years, and had moved up to second place with 207, only two strokes away from Arnold. Dow had only 24 putts in his round; he used an old putter with a new hickory shaft.

The final day's pairing of Arnold Palmer and Gary Player added greatly to the excitement of the finish. Palmer started right out by failing to hole makeable putts on the first and second holes (a 20-incher on the latter) and at the short fourth hole he completely missed his 1-iron moving the ball only 125 yards off the tee. He missed a six-foot putt at No. 7 and his lead had evaporated. Finsterwald was playing well ahead of Palmer and Player and early in their play on the back nine, they both knew they had a total of 280 strokes to tie or beat when Finsterwald's score of 73 was posted.

Arnold double-bogied the tenth hole and fell two strokes behind Player (as well as behind Finsterwald's 280 complete score).

Palmer was able to recover his composure, stayed at par on the back nine as Gary matched him stroke for stroke until the sixteenth where a dramatic 45-foot hooded wedge chip-shot from the right edge of the green found the flagstick and disappeared into the cup for a much-needed deuce for Arnold. Player made his par at No. 16 and was then only one stroke ahead of Palmer at this time and needed pars in to tie Finsterwald.

On No. 17 Arnold hit a magnificent 8 iron to within 12 feet of the flag. Then he calmly sank the putt for his birdie to set up the eventual three-way tie between himself, Player, and Finsterwald. Both Palmer and Player had putts for the outright win at the eighteenth green but neither could find the cup.

In the playoff, Palmer very nearly duplicated the script of his previous round. He played badly for the first nine holes and fell three strokes behind Player. Finsterwald, meanwhile, was never in contention and took a 77 for the round.

Then, Palmer struck back again with the lightning his army of followers had come to expect. Arnold birdied Nos. 10 and 12, two-putted No. 13 for a birdie, and followed with a 16-foot birdie putt on No. 14. In those five holes, Player's game fell off and Arnie had gone from three strokes down to four strokes ahead.

It was Palmer 68, Player 71, Finisterwald 77. For Palmer, it was his third Masters, and the win certainly gave him great personal satisfaction over his comeback from near disaster.

33
The Masters of 1963

1963

Jack Nicklaus	74	66	74	72	286
Tony Lema	74	69	74	70	287
Julius Boros	76	69	71	72	288
Sam Snead	70	73	74	71	288
Dow Finsterwald	74	73	73	69	289
Ed Furgol	70	71	74	74	289
Gary Player	71	74	74	70	289
Bo Wininger	69	72	77	72	290
Don January	73	75	72	71	291
Arnold Palmer	74	73	73	71	291

Arnold Palmer, again the favorite, found himself in a tie for fourteenth place with an opening score of 74. The wind blew in gusts up to 35 miles an hour and the greens baked out in a hot sun as scores soared. There were 17 scores in the 80s and four players reported "no cards."

Jack Nicklaus, the U. S. Open Champion (victor over Arnold Palmer at Oakmont in 1962) was paired with long-hitting George Bayer. Jack three-putted twice on the way to a 74, five strokes off the pace set by Bo Wininger and Mike Souchak who had 69s.

On the second day, Mike Souchak retained his lead on a fine 70 for a 36-hole total of 139, but the threat of Jack Nicklaus began to become apparent. Playing in his fourth Masters tourney, Jack did not make a serious error in a six-under-par 66 and went into second place with 140. The wind had died away and playing conditions were excellent.

Jack Nicklaus became the youngest Masters Champion in history when he won this tournament with a closing 72 for 286 and the $20,000 prize. Tony Lema had already finished ahead of Jack and by sinking a 25-foot curling putt at the home hole put the pressure on Jack, who was playing behind him. Julius Boros and Sam Snead were at 288 and Gary Player, Dow Finsterwald, and Ed Furgol were at 289—close to catching Jack Nicklaus.

Jack appeared to be in trouble at the eighteenth hole. Needing a par there to win by one stroke, he hooked his drive into a muddy area much trampled by the crowd. He was fortunate to obtain an official ruling that he was in "casual water" and thus entitled to drop away from the spot into a drier place. He did so and lofted a high pitch to the green safely. He left himself a testy three-footer, but calmly put the ball in the hole to win his first Masters Championship.

Jack Nicklaus, winner in 1963, 1965, 1966 and 1972.

34
The Masters of 1964

1964

Arnold Palmer	69	68	69	70	276
Dave Marr	70	73	69	70	282
Jack Nicklaus	71	73	71	67	282
Bruce Devlin	72	72	67	73	284
Billy Casper, Jr.	76	72	69	69	286
Jim Ferrier	71	73	69	73	286
Paul Harney	73	72	71	70	286
Gary Player	69	72	72	73	286
Dow Finsterwald	71	72	75	69	287
Ben Hogan	73	75	67	72	287
Tony Lema	75	68	74	70	287
Mike Souchak	73	74	70	70	287

Tony Lema and Arnold Palmer were among the favorites in the 1964 Masters Tournament.

Gary Player, facing a tonsillectomy, was not up to his usual fine state of physical fitness. Rains had slowed the course so the word was out to watch out for the long hitters, Nicklaus and Palmer.

At the end of the first day, Palmer was clustered with a group of four others—Goalby, Love, Nagle, and Player—at 69. Only Player would end up in the top ten and he would be ten strokes away from the eventual winner.

When the dust had settled on the second round's shooting, Arnold Palmer had brought in another sub-par round, this time a 68, and although Tony Lema also scored a 68, Arnold was already four strokes ahead of the field. Gary Player was riding in second on a 69–72, 141 halfway count.

Arnold Palmer birdied four of the last six holes in getting his 68 and had hit a 1 iron to the thirteenth green on his second shot, which left him five feet from the hole. The "eagle" became a birdie when he rimmed the putt. Tony Lema did make his eagle at No. 13, however, on a 3 iron to fifteen feet from the cup.

On the third day, the script remained the same, as Palmer took a five-stroke lead on another great 69 for a 206 total at 54 holes. Before the largest crowd in Masters history, estimated to have been 40,000 people, Palmer birdied Nos. 14, 15, and 16. Bruce Devlin, Australian Amateur Champion in 1960 and winner of the Australian Open while still an amateur, made a strong move toward catching Palmer when he registered an excellent 67 and moved to second position at 211, five shots behind the leader.

On the last day, Palmer won with ease by six strokes when he scored a 70 for a 276 total, only two strokes away from Ben Hogan's low record total of 274 in the 1953 Masters. Palmer was in trouble twice on his last round, once at No. 11 where he hooked a 3 iron into the water and scored a bogey 5 and at No. 13 where he again hooked, this time into the trees on the left. He "saved" this hole by getting out of the woods with a wedge and then screamed a 4 iron to the green for a saving par.

Arnold Palmer thus became the first four-time winner of the Masters, surpassing Jimmy Demaret's record of three victories in 1940, 1947, and 1950 and Sam Snead's record of three victories in 1949, 1952, and 1954.

35
The Masters of 1965

1965

Jack Nicklaus	67	71	64	69	271
Arnold Palmer	70	68	72	70	280
Gary Player	65	73	69	73	280
Mason Rudolph	70	75	66	72	283
Dan Sikes	67	72	71	75	285
Gene Littler	71	74	67	74	286
Ramon Sota	71	73	70	72	286
Frank Beard	68	77	72	70	287
Tommy Bolt	69	78	69	71	287
George Knudson	72	73	69	74	288

The year 1965 was the one in which Jack Nicklaus took the Augusta National golf course apart. Jack blasted the Masters field with a third-round 64, tying Lloyd Mangrum's course record set in 1940, and setting a new 54-hole record of 202, three shots better than Ben Hogan's previous record of 205 set in 1953. The longest club Jack used on a par 4 was a 6-iron. At the eighth hole, the 530 yard 5 par, he was home with a 3-iron. The third round had started with a three-way tie between Nicklaus, Palmer, and Player at 138.

On the last day, Nicklaus scored the most one-sided victory ever accomplished in the Masters with a 69 finish for a record-shattering total of 271. Jack finished nine strokes ahead of his competitors. His 64 had put him five strokes ahead of Player and eight strokes ahead of Palmer. Player and

Palmer ended in a deadlock for second place with 280, Player had a final 73 and Palmer a 70.

The winning margin of nine strokes beat Cary Middlecoff's record seven-stroke margin in 1955. The weather was clear and the greens "fast." Nicklaus's putting was keen and consistently accurate. His putting total for the four days was 123 on individual putting rounds of 32, 31, 30 and 30. He had 19 birdies and went over par 5 times in the four days. Nicklaus received $20,000 as first prize money. The overall purse was $140,075, $10,275 more than the year before.

Bill Casper took a 6 at the eleventh by getting into the creek and then took 8 on the twelfth. He went into the pond twice and then overshot the green into a bunker. Casper ended with 80 after a 72–72–71 start and finished far down the list with 295. Mason Rudolph was fourth at 283, Dan Sikes fifth at 285, and Spanish entrant Ramon Sota tied with Gene Littler for sixth at 286.

Jack Nicklaus's Record 64 in 1965

This is the story of Jack Nicklaus' record-tying 64 in his third round of the 1965 Masters. It is taken from an interview with Jack on September 29, 1971, and is quoted with his permission:

"I remember that my tee-shot on No. 1 was downwind, although there was very little wind that day. I hit it so far I used a wedge to the green. The pin was on the front left-hand side and I couldn't hold the ball near it. I ended up on the back edge of the green about 40 feet away. I "trolled" my putt to within one inch of the cup and made 4.

On No. 2, I hit a bad drive, pretty far, but way into the trees on the right, about 60 feet from the fairway. I think I hit a 3-iron through the opening to about 50 yards short of the green. My putt was 20 feet or so downhill and the green was extremely fast. I just touched the putt and it rolled and rolled and finally just toppled into the hole for the birdie 4.

On No. 3, I hit a 3-wood off the tee short of the bunker in the middle of the fairway and wedged to 8 feet away. Did not make the putt, par 4.

We were playing the "short tee" on No. 4 that day, that would be about between the present back tee and the lower front tee. I hit my 4-iron "fat" and was disgusted with the shot. A photographer took my picture when I made a terrible face. But the shot made the green and rolled to about 10 feet away from the hole. The cup was in the front left center. I made the 2 for another birdie. The putt had a left-to-right bend.

On No. 5, a drive and 6-iron and two putts from 20 feet. Nothing unusual.

On No. 6, I hit a 6-iron to 20 feet above the cup, which was on the front left side of the green. Again it was a very slick situation, but I made the 2.

On the seventh hole, I hit a wedge two feet from the hole and made an easy 3.

I hit a very long drive on No. 8 and then a 3-iron which ended up on the green but 75 feet from the hole. I two-putted for a birdie 4.

At No. 9, I hit a long drive and wedge to about 20 feet from the hole, took two putts for the par 4 and 31 on the nine.

On No. 10, I hit a drive to the right-hand side of the fairway. You know that's where you shouldn't hit it, because it makes the hole a lot longer. But I still had only an 8-iron to the green. I made the green 20 feet from the hole and two-putted for the par 4.

Again, on No. 11, I hit my drive pretty long but on the right side. The pin was on the left-hand side of the green. I got on the green but about 50 feet from the hole. I two-putted for the par 4.

At No. 12, the pin was on the front left side of the green. I hit an 8-iron to 4 feet away and missed the birdie.

On No. 13, I hooked my drive around the corner and hit a 5-iron just barely on the green, took two putts from 45 feet for the birdie 4. [The film of the Masters of 1965 shows that Jack nearly three-putted this green. His first putt left him about 8 feet short and with a slippery downhill putt to make. His putt just barely toppled into the cup to save his birdie there.]

On No. 14, I drove into the rough again, this time on the right side of the fairway. I hit a 7-iron to 25 feet and took two putts for the par 4.

I hit a very long drive on No. 15, about 325 yards but into the left rough so that I was blocked by trees on my second shot. I couldn't hit straight for the pin, which was on the left side of the green. I hit a 5-iron to the back right fringe, chipped a 6-iron to 18 inches, and made the putt. I remember that the chip was really a great one, that it kept rolling and rolling closer and closer to the pin.

At No. 16, I hit a 6-iron to 14 feet from the hole. I remember the pin was in exactly the same position and the putt was from exactly the same place as it was when I made a birdie 2 in 1963 and went on to win the Masters. It broke about six inches, right to left. I made the putt again for a birdie 2.

No. 17 was rather routine. I drove very far and hit an 8-iron to the front fringe. I putted from the fringe, put it close, and holed for the par 4.

I hit a very long drive way up the fairway. Remember, this was before the trap was put in the center of the fairway where it can catch your drive. The pin was down in the lower front right and my second shot, with my wedge, went about 25 feet beyond the hole. I two-putted for the par 4, had a 33 on the last nine and a total of 64. There were 8 birdies and 10 pars, not one 5 on the scorecard."

36
The Masters of 1966

1966

Jack Nicklaus	68	76	72	72	288
Play off					70
Tommy Jacobs	75	71	70	72	288
Play off					72
Gay Brewer, Jr.	74	72	72	70	288
Play off					78
Arnold Palmer	74	70	74	72	290
Doug Sanders	74	70	75	71	290
Don January	71	73	73	75	292
George Knudson	73	76	72	71	292
Raymond L. Floyd	72	73	74	74	293
Paul Harney	75	68	76	74	293
Billy Casper, Jr.	71	75	76	72	294
Jay Hebert	72	74	73	75	294
Bob Rosburg	73	71	76	74	294

Gay Brewer, Tommy Jacobs, and Jack Nicklaus finished in a three-way tie at the end of the regulation 72 holes of the Masters of 1966. Brewer missed a 7-foot putt for a par 4 on the 18th hole. He had a sidehill 40 footer from the back of the green and tried to lag it close enough to get down in two but the ball slipped seven feet beyond the cup. Although he hit his second putt firmly, the ball broke more than he expected.

Nicklaus and Jacobs shared the lead at the end of the third round and each shot a 72 in the final round while Brewer came in with a 70. The three tied at 288, a 72-hole aggregate only one stroke

less than the record high when Jack Burke won with a 289. Hogan and Snead also tied at that figure in 1954 before Snead won in the playoff.

Jack Nicklaus missed a 3½-foot putt for a birdie at No. 17 as Jacobs and Brewer, who had already completed their rounds, awaited Jack's finish at No. 18. On the eighteenth Jack had a downhill, sidehill 40 footer that just barely missed the cup or Jack would have won the tournament outright.

In the playoff, Nicklaus and Jacobs each went out in 35 while Brewer stumbled to a 38. Jacobs started out the playoff round strongly with a birdie 3 to take an early lead but Jack Nicklaus caught him with a birdie at the second hole where Jack's 3-wood second shot struck the pin on the fly and bounced 30 feet away. Jacobs went ahead again at the fourth where Nicklaus was bunkered and took 4 but Jack made a downhill 18-foot putt on No. 6 for a deuce to draw even again. Both played the ninth badly for bogies. Jack picked up two strokes on Jacobs on Nos. 10 and 11 with 4–3 against Jacobs's 5–4. Jack holed a 25-foot putt for his birdie at No. 11. They matched each other's cards all the rest of the way for 37s and 70–72 totals while Brewer was never in contention. He took 40 strokes on the second nine including a double-bogey 6 at the seventeenth hole.

Jack Nicklaus became the first Masters champion to succeed himself.

37
The Masters of 1967

1967

Gay Brewer, Jr.	73	68	72	67	280
Bobby Nichols	72	69	70	70	281
Bert Yancey	67	73	71	73	284
Arnold Palmer	73	73	70	69	285
Julius Boros	71	70	70	75	286
Paul Harney	73	71	74	69	287
Gary Player	75	69	72	71	287
Tommy Aaron	75	68	74	71	288
Lionel Hebert	77	71	67	73	288
Roberto de Vicenzo	73	72	74	71	290
Bruce Devlin	74	70	75	71	290
Ben Hogan	74	73	66	77	290
Mason Rudolph	72	76	72	70	290
Sam Snead	72	76	71	71	290

1967 winner, Gay Brewer, Jr.

This was the year that Gay Brewer redeemed himself for failing to win the Masters of 1966. He scored a magnificent 67 in a final round played with his closest pursuer and good friend, Bobby Nichols, who scored a 70 to finish one stroke behind Gay, 280 to 281. Brewer had three straight birdies on the last nine holes in his final round, at Nos. 13, 14, and 15. A crucial exchange occurred at the uphill fourteenth where Nichols had a makeable putt for a birdie that would have put him into a tie with Gay should Gay miss his 20-foot birdie attempt. Gay holed his putt and then Bobby holed his as well to remain one stroke behind.

Bert Yancey, 28 years old and playing in his first Masters, made an impressive start and was considered to be the possible winner after the first two days' play. Bert started out with 67 in the first round and took a three-stroke lead over Billy Casper and Amateur Downing Gray, who had scores of 70. Jack Nicklaus opened with a par 72, and when he followed with a poor 79, found himself in the unenviable position of being the only former champion who did not qualify for the last two rounds of play.

Yancey kept the lead on the second day with a 73 for a 140 total as Gay Brewer started his move toward the eventual championship. Gay scored a 68, after his first-round 73. Julius Boros, Tony Jacklin, and Bobby Nichols were also in very close pursuit at 141. Incidentally, this was Tony Jacklin's first appearance at the Augusta National course. He had gained his invitation when Neil Coles, ahead of Tony on the English "select list," decided to forego the tournament.

The third round was highlighted by the electricity of Ben Hogan's remarkable 66, a score which he personally had equalled only once at Augusta, in 1953, when he captured the British Open and the United States Open Championships in that same year.

At the end of the third day, Boros, Nichols, and Yancey all shared a three-way tie for the lead at 211 strokes, while Gay Brewer was only two strokes back of the leaders. Hogan had begun his third round eight strokes behind Nichols and had pulled up to a tie with Brewer, two strokes away from the top. Hogan's day was over, however, as he finished with a tired 77 for a tie at tenth place.

Gay Brewer carded a final round of 67 for a 280 total to win by one stroke over Bobby Nichols, who had a 70 for 281 and second place all alone. Brewer and Nichols were paired together on the final day to the pleasure of the galleries. Brewer won the tournament by shooting those three straight birdies on the back nine.

After he had won, Brewer said, "I think I redeemed myself," meaning that he felt that he had atoned for his failure to win the year before.

One of the most heart-warming scenes in the history of golf happened in mid-afternoon of the third day of the 1967 Masters. The "wee ice mon," Ben Hogan, as the Scots had called him at Carnoustie when he won their prized Open Championship so coolly in 1953, came back to life again for four hours at the Augusta National Golf Course. After missing several Masters, as a result of illness, and putting in token appearances in several more, Ben Hogan returned to his old form this particular day. Out in a respectable 36 strokes on the first nine, he gave no sign of the fireworks he intended to show on the second nine.

At the tenth hole he placed a 7-iron 7 feet from the cup and sank his putt for a birdie 3. A roar went up at the main scoreboard near the eighteenth green as Ben's 3 was recorded and some of the spectators left to head down into the "Amen Corner." Perhaps Ben could still play golf in his old style and would be interesting to watch.

At the eleventh a 6-iron stopped 12 inches from the ball and Ben had birdie 2 on the second nine. Again, a roar went up when his score was posted at the huge scoreboard. His crowd again increased in numbers.

But Ben did not stop there. He put a 6-iron within 15 feet of the twelfth flagstick and down went the putt for a 2. Three birdies in a row! And the 5-par thirteenth, eminently birdieable was coming up next. A drive, a comfortable 4-wood to 20 feet from the hole, and Ben had made a "normal" birdie 4 for his fourth birdie in a row. The roars of the crowds at the scoreboards in every corner of the golf course became louder and louder as the red numbers went up after Ben's name on hole after hole. Could Ben keep up that torrid pace? He did. A par at No. 14 brought him to another possible birdie hole.

Again, a typical long straight Hogan drive left him a 4-wood away from another birdie opportunity. The tremendous crowd now following him held its collective breath as he dared to carry the water in front of the fifteenth green. Over the water and 20 feet from the hole, the ball came to rest. There followed two putts and Ben Hogan had his fifth birdie of the nine. Could he keep on going? Would his tired legs give out on him? The sixteenth and seventeenth fell to Ben in normal pars, on the green in regulation strokes and two putts for the pars.

To the eighteenth, the tough uphill finishing hole, with the blind pin position. Now there were between ten and twelve thousand people lining both sides of the eighteenth fairway, hoping for Ben, praying that he could solve the last hole in par. A birdie would be miraculous, of course. Ben's tee-shot was straight and just short of the dangerous mid-fairway bunker. Without any hesitation, he cracked a sweet 5-iron up the hill to the plateau green now completely surrounded by the massed gallery.

The ball carried the bunker in front of the green and came to a skidding stop 25 feet from the hole, too far away, everyone thought, to hope for a birdie. Then poor tired Ben Hogan began to climb that last 160 yards uphill to the last green. The galleries came to life. They realized that they were seeing a living legend, one of the greatest golfers of all time, proving his courage and his skill in one last magnificent effort of concentration.and perfect execution of the golf swing.

The roars of the crowd started as he passed the center fairway bunker. They increased in intensity as Ben laboriously placed one foot down after the other in his climb up the hill. It takes four minutes for a man in good health to climb that hill. I think it took Ben Hogan five minutes for I was there to see the scene and to feel the drama unfolding. He tipped his little white visored cap several times as he neared the green. Whether there were tears in his eyes, we will never know, but I suspect that the great golfer's heart melted at this thundering unending display of admiration.

Of course, he rolled that 25 foot putt right into the hole for his sixth birdie and a course record score of 30 strokes. Do you think his guardian angel would have allowed him to miss that putt? I don't.

38
The Masters of 1968

1968

Bob Goalby	70	70	71	66	277
Roberto de Vicenzo	69	73	70	66	278
Bert Yancey	71	71	72	65	279
Bruce Devlin	69	73	69	69	280
Frank Beard	75	65	71	70	281
Jack Nicklaus	69	71	74	67	281
Gary Player	72	67	71	72	282
Raymond Floyd	71	71	69	71	282
Tommy Aaron	69	72	72	69	282
Jerry Pittman	70	73	70	69	282
Lionel Hebert	72	71	71	68	282

The year 1968 was the one of the "wrong score-card" incident at the Masters, an unfortunate occurrence which cost Roberto de Vicenzo a tie for the Championship of that year and allowed Bob Goalby to don the green winner's coat as undisputed champion.

The golf course at Augusta National was once again rain-drenched and slow as the play began with the smallest field in years, only 74 players. Billy Casper had won in Greensboro and was on his game. It was apparent, too, for on the first day, Casper used only 29 putts in a fine 68 to take the early lead in the tournament. Tommy Aaron, Roberto de Vicenzo, Jack Nicklaus, and Bruce Devlin were at 69. Bob Goalby, in the first pairing of the day after 86-year-old Fred McLeod and 83-year-old Jock Hutchinson had started the field in

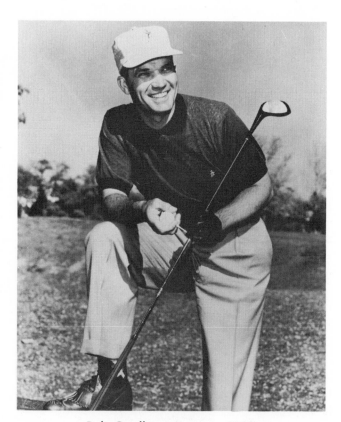

Bob Goalby, winner in 1968.

traditional fashion, was unnoticed behind the clustered leaders with a sound 70.

On the second day, there were nine players in a bunch from Don January and Gary Player at 139 to de Vicenzo, Devlin and Floyd at 142. Goalby, still not in the spotlight, had put together two 70s now to be only one stroke off the leaders' pace. Arnold Palmer missed the 36 hole cutoff after a 79, which included a horrendous 8 at the fifteenth hole. Bruce Devlin at one time was leading the field by three strokes until he, too, took an 8 on the eleventh hole.

It was apparent that the tournament was a wide-open one, with no one so far ready to establish a firm grip on the leadership.

Going into the last round the field remained in a tight cluster. The scoreboard showed:

Player	72	67	71	210
Beard	75	65	71	211
Devlin	69	73	69	211
Floyd	71	71	69	211
Goalby	70	70	71	211
January	71	68	72	211
de Vicenzo	69	73	70	212
Trevino	71	72	69	212

Bob Goalby emerged from this jam of great golfers with a magnificent 66. Bob was playing behind the pairing of de Vicenzo and Tommy Aaron and was able to birdie the thirteenth hole with an 8-foot putt and the fourteenth hole on a 15-foot putt, and eagle the fifteenth when he stroked a 3-iron within 8 feet of the cup and sank the putt to go 12 under par for the tournament.

Roberto de Vicenzo had started out brilliantly ahead of Bob Goalby. At the first hole, Roberto sank his second shot for an opening eagle 2. Later on he birdied No. 12 for a 2, No. 13 for a 4, No. 15 for another 4. He had 31 strokes on the outward nine and finished with what appeared to be a 65, bogeying No. 18 on a shot into the crowd there surrounding the green.

The scoreboards were then showing de Vicenzo apparently 11 under par so when Goalby, playing behind de Vicenzo, three-putted the seventeenth hole, it was evident that he needed to par the eighteenth hole for an apparent tie with Roberto de Vicenzo. A National Television audience had watched de Vicenzo sink a five-foot putt on the seventeenth hole for what they thought was the birdie three to put de Vicenzo into the 11 under

par situation and on the way to a tie with Goalby, that is, provided that Goalby could par the eighteenth hole.

Goalby managed to sink a tricky 5-foot putt for his par 4 and a great round of 66 for a total score of 277. The scorecards were signed by the scorers of the twosomes, Tommy Aaron for de Vicenzo and de Vicenzo for Aaron as is customary in golf tournaments run under the rules of the United States Golf Association, the Masters tournament being one of them.

Suddenly, before the national television audience, it was clear that something had gone wrong. The usual speeches and presentations were being delayed.

Then, it was announced that the de Vicenzo scorecard attested by Tommy Aaron and countersigned as correct had reported a 4 as de Vicenzo's score on the seventeenth hole, not the 3 the millions of television viewers had seen him make.

Furthermore, under the Rules of Golf, unfortunate as the circumstances were, Homer E. Shields, the tournament director, declared that de Vicenzo's score was a 66, not the 65 everyone thought he had scored, that his total score was therefore 278, which left him one stroke behind Goalby, runnerup and not tied with Goalby for the championship.

The official U.S.G.A. Rule 38, Paragraph 3, specifies that: "No alteration may be made on a card after the competitor has returned it to the Committee. If the competitor return a score for any hole lower than actually played, he shall be disqualified. A score higher than actually played must stand as returned."

Roberto de Vicenzo was quoted in the newspapers as having said enroute to the television area, "I just signed a wrong card. The other fellow (Tommy Aaron) put down a 4. It's my fault." Robert de Vicenzo made millions of friends in the golf world by his gracious acceptance of this regrettable occurrence which cost him the chance of a lifetime to be a Masters Champion. Bob Goalby, under the circumstances totally beyond his own control, became sole and undisputed Masters Champion of 1968.

39
The Masters of 1969

1969

George Archer	67	73	69	72	281
Bill Casper	66	71	71	74	282
George Knudson	70	73	69	70	282
Tom Weiskopf	71	71	69	71	282
Charles Coody	74	68	69	72	283
Don January	74	73	70	66	283
Miller Barber	71	71	68	74	284
Tommy Aaron	71	71	73	70	285
Lionel Hebert	69	73	70	73	285
Gene Littler	69	75	70	71	285

George Archer, Masters winner in 1969.

Billy Casper, Jr., started the 1969 Masters with a sparkling 66 and at the end of the first day it appeared that this Masters might have one of the lowest scoring fields in its history. Sundown of the first day found George Archer at 67 and no less than six players at 69, Gene Littler, Lionel Hebert, Mason Rudolph, Dan Sikes, Bert Yancey and Bruce Crampton.

And who was this George Archer in second place? A tall 6-foot, 6-inch former California Amateur Champion who had recently turned Professional and had won the Pensacola and New Orleans Open Championship in 1968. George was considered a long-shot to win this Masters, especially when Billy Casper was apparently taking complete charge of the situation this April. For Bill had followed up his great 66 beginning with a 71 to be co-leader at the halfway mark and on another 71 was leading the field all alone as he began his last round.

Both George Archer and Charles Coody, however, climbed into contention on third-round 69s and were riding at 209 and 211, respectively one and three strokes behind Casper.

Casper had a most unfortunate first nine, actually ten, holes on the last day. He had scored only two bogeys in all three of his previous rounds and incredibly, in a sudden reversal of form racked up five bogies in ten holes to be five over par for the round.

In the meantime both Coody and Archer were playing steady, if not spectacular golf. When Coody laced a 2-iron to within 25 feet of the thirteenth hole and downed the putt for an eagle 3 he went 8 under par for the whole tournament and one stroke ahead of George Archer, who was playing just behind him.

Casper was making a comeback, too; he got a birdie at No. 11 and two brave 4s at the five-par thirteenth and fifteenth in an attempt to salvage what had appeared to be the best chance he had ever had to win his first Masters tournament.

Archer also birdied the thirteenth hole to pull even with Coody. Coody bogied No. 14 and then promptly recovered from that mistake with a good birdie at No. 15. Actually, Coody took the sole lead at this point when Archer also bogied No. 14.

Then Coody's game went to pieces and he stumbled in with three straight bogies on the last three holes.

Archer, now coming on strong, could sense his chance to win. A crucial situation occurred when Archer's second shot at the watery fifteenth found the pond. Archer calmly pitched over the wafer and sank a 10-foot putt to save his par there. He came in with three straight pars, including a very comfortable one at the eighteenth hole, where his second shot landed only 12 feet from the cup. He putted to a few inches away from the cup, sank the next putt and was the new Masters Champion. He had scored a 281, seven strokes under Augusta National's par. It took a size 42 "extra long" green coat to fit George Archer, the tallest Champion in Masters history.

There was a three-way tie for second place among George Knudson of Canada, who finished his last two rounds with 69–70; Tom Weiskopf, who had 69–71; and Billy Casper, Jr., who almost salvaged his bad start with a 34 back nine and a round of 74 strokes. Billy had an unsuccessful 30-yard chip for a birdie at No. 18 or he might have tied George Archer after all. It was just not Billy Casper's year to win the Masters. But, wait 'til next year and he'd show 'em!

40
The Masters of 1970

1970

Bill Casper	72	68	68	71	279
Play off					69
Gene Littler	69	70	70	70	279
Play off					74
Gary Player	74	68	68	70	280
Bert Yancey	69	70	72	70	281
Tommy Aaron	68	74	69	72	283
Dave Hill	73	70	70	70	283
Dave Stockton	72	72	69	70	283
Jack Nicklaus	71	75	69	69	284
Frank Beard	71	76	68	70	285
Bob Lunn	70	70	75	72	287
Juan Rodriguez	70	76	73	68	287

1970 winner, Billy Casper.

The 1970 Masters was one of the most suspenseful tournaments in recent years. During the play on the last day, at one moment in time there were seven players within one or two strokes of the lead and of each other: Billy Casper, Jr., Gene Littler, Gary Player, Bert Yancey, Dave Hill, Dave Stockton, and Tommy Aaron. Each one of them had an excellent chance, but when it came down to the final putts on the eighteenth hole, Billy Casper and Gene Littler found themselves in a tie at 279 strokes and thus entered the sixth playoff in Masters history.

On the first day Tommy Aaron was off to a one-stroke lead over the field on a great 68. Close behind were Littler and Yancey at 69. Casper had a sound 72 and followed with a strong 68. Littler was back the second day with a 70. So, at the halfway mark, there were Littler at 139, Yancey at 139 (having matched Gene's 69–70), Casper at 140, Aaron and Player at 142.

Casper, putting phenomenally all the way, kept saving pars on one-putts when he wasn't making them conventionally. Littler remained steady and came in with a third-round 70. Casper's 68 gave him a one-stroke lead at 208 to Gene's 209. Player had moved up on a 68 to 210 to set the stage for the dramatic finale on Sunday. With only nine holes to play, Casper, Littler, and Yancey were tied for the lead and Player was one stroke behind.

Casper had shown signs of weakening and no doubt had memories of his sagging finish in 1969 to lose that tournament to George Archer. Billy had hit his drive into the right-hand bunker at No. 8 and had taken a double-bogey there. However, he managed to run down a long birdie putt at No. 9 and get some of his confidence back.

Casper and Littler both birdied No. 13 and showed the strength coming down the stretch. Casper made a necessary and typical save for his 4 at No. 15 to match Littler's birdie there a few minutes ahead of him. Both Casper and Littler had possible winning birdie putts at both No. 17 and No. 18, but neither man was able to hole the ball and win the title outright. Their scores of 71 and 70 gave them each a 279 total for the four rounds.

Player stumbled to a bogey 5 at No. 18 after hooking his second shot into the bunker, and was out of the race when he missed his putt for the par. He took third place at 280. In the meantime, Yancey had failed to get his birdie at No. 15 when the others did and when he, too, bogeyed No. 18 he fell behind Gary Player and finished at 281 in fourth place.

The playoff between Casper and Littler was anticlimactic. Both men played erratically and sometimes badly, but Casper, as usual, saved himself with his magic putting stroke. He registered six one-putt greens in the first seven holes, was then three under par and in the lead over Gene by five strokes. The second hole was a turning point in the match when Littler dubbed his third, a little wedge shot, only ten feet into a bunker.

Casper saved his par there after being in trouble at the start of the hole and was never headed during the rest of the match. Casper shot 69 to Littler's 74 in the playoff. Billy Casper, Jr., National Open champion of 1959 had finally won the Masters.

41
The Masters of 1971

1971

Charles Coody	66	73	70	70	279
John Miller	72	73	68	68	281
Jack Nicklaus	70	71	68	72	281
Don January	69	69	73	72	283
Gene Littler	72	69	73	69	283
Gary Player	72	72	71	69	284
Ken Still	72	71	72	69	284
Tom Weiskopf	71	69	72	72	284
Frank Beard	74	73	69	70	286
Roberto de Vicenzo	76	69	72	69	286
Dave Stockton	72	73	69	72	286

Charles Coody became the 34th Masters champion, winning by two strokes over young John Miller and formidable Jack Nicklaus, with scores of 279 to 281.

Jack Nicklaus had already won the P.G.A. Championship (played earlier this year in an experiment by the Professional Golf Association to increase public interest in the event) and was attempting to take the second part of his much desired "grand slam." The year before, after being in the lead with only three holes to play, Charles Coody had finished with three consecutive bogies to lose the coveted Championship and fall into a tie for fifth place. This year he wanted badly to prove that he could win the Championship. On the first day, Coody opened with a par 36 first nine and then fashioned a beautiful 32 on the second

Charles Coody, winner in 1971.

nine for a sparkling 66, which brought him a three-shot lead over the field. He birdied Nos. 10, 13, 14, and 15 on the way to this great start. In the meantime, Nicklaus and Miller were off with 72 and 70 respectively. There was a five-way tie at 69 among Don January, Ray Floyd, Bob Lunn, Bob Murphy, and Hale Irwin. Only January fulfilled this promising beginning, as he finished in 69–73–72 for 283 and a tie for fourth place with Gene Littler who had 72–69–73–69 for his 283.

Coody slumped a bit on his second round, shooting a 73. Out in a shaky 39 strokes he lost another stroke to par at the short twelfth, but again accomplished a birdie spree at Nos. 13, 15, and 16 to "save" the round with a 33 back nine. Nicklaus had a 71 and picked up two valuable strokes on Coody.

Coody came back with a 70 on the third day while Jack closed up the stroke margin with a 68. They went into the third round tied at 209. In the meantime John Miller, by scoring a fine 68 on his third round, came within two strokes of the leaders at the start of the final round, 211 to 213.

Miller started the last day and proceeded to burn up the course. He scored three birdies on the first nine and then three more on the second nine at the eleventh, twelfth, and fourteenth holes to put himself 9 under par and to lead the field at that time by two strokes over Coody and Nicklaus with only four holes to play. But John bunkered his second shot at a birdie hole, No. 15, and scored no better than par. Then he stumbled to two more bogeys at Nos. 16 and 18 and his chances were gone.

Meanwhile, Coody had followed Miller and with a birdie at No. 15 cut Miller's margin to one stroke. When Coody stroked a sweet iron to 15 feet from the sixteenth flagstick and then holed the putt, the lead had changed hands. Nicklaus, like Miller, failed to birdie No. 15. His 4-iron went over the green and his chip left him too far away for the birdie.

Now leading both Nicklaus and Miller by two strokes, Coody scrambled to a chip and 7-foot putt to save his par at No. 17. With a two-stroke lead at No. 18, Coody was able to make his par at the final hole and a few minutes later Billy Casper, 1970 Masters Champion, raised Charles Coody's arm in triumph after he had helped him don his green Masters coat. The 1970 Masters had truly been avenged by Charles Coody.

42
The Masters of 1972

1972

Jack Nicklaus	68	71	73	74	286
Bruce Crampton	72	75	69	73	289
Tom Weiskopf	74	71	70	74	289
Bobby Mitchell	73	72	71	73	289
Jim Jamieson	72	70	71	77	290
Homero Blancas	76	71	69	74	290
Jerry Heard	73	71	72	74	290
Bruce Devlin	74	75	70	71	290
Jerry McGee	73	74	71	72	290
Gary Player	73	75	72	71	291
Dave Stockton	76	70	74	71	291

Jack Nicklaus tied Arnold Palmer's record of winning four Masters Championships when he added the 1972 Masters title to his impressive record of eleven major golf championships and achieved the first leg of the "Grand Slam" of golf, the United States and British Open Championships, the Professional Golf Association Championship and the Masters.

Jack started out slowly in his first round. He was in and out of trouble on the first nine for a one over par 37. When he bogeyed the tenth hole, he appeared to be in even more difficulty. In the meantime, defending champion Charles Coody had started off well. To the delight of his followers, he had scored a hole-in-one on the hard three-par sixth hole to put himself four under par and be-

come the leader of the field at that time. But Coody had trouble extricating himself from the sand of the front bunker at the seventh hole and took a horrendous 7 there, three over par. He was never in contention again.

Nicklaus started his move toward the lead with a remarkable stretch of fine golf beginning with the eleventh hole which he birdied. At the twelfth hole he sank a 25 footer for a birdie 2. At thirteen, he hit a 3-wood from the tee and a 6-iron to the left bunker, recovered nicely to 3 feet and had another birdie. He parred No. 14 normally. No. 15 fell to him in 3 strokes, an eagle, when he hit a long drive and a 235-yard 1-iron shot to within 30 feet of the cup. Jack holed his birdie 2 from the fringe of No. 16 as the galleries became hysterical with delight. He had played the last six holes in 6 under par.

At this point, Jack Nicklaus moved past aging Sam Snead who had played magnificently only to falter a bit with his putter and end at 69 to Jack's leading score of 68.

Jack was never headed from then on. Several players made moves as if they were going to catch him. Jim Jamieson, a young newcomer in his first Masters, played extremely well through three rounds of 72–70–71, but could only manage 77 on the last day. Bruce Crampton, Bobby Mitchell,

Lee Trevino punches an iron.

Paul Harney at the thirteenth green.

The intense concentration of Gary Player as he attempts a bunker shot. Gary is acknowledged to be one of the best bunker shot-makers in the game.

Roberto de Vicenzo in trouble at the ninth.

Gary Player comes out of trouble as usual, close to the hole.

"The Old Squire," Gene Sarazen, again retells the story of his double-eagle on the fifteenth hole.

Sam Snead, the veteran campaigner, looks at his millionth tee-shot problem.

"Jumbo," Musashi Ozaki, hits one of his tremendous drives.

and Tom Weiskopf closed with 73,73,74, respectively, to share a tie for second place at 289, three strokes behind Jack Nicklaus's conservative 74. If Jack had not had trouble with the fifteenth hole, where he scored double bogeys on his third and fourth rounds, he might have broken open the tournament as decisively as he did when he won in 1965 by nine strokes.

The low amateur was 20-year-old Ben Crenshaw, who scored a very creditable 295 to tie for nineteenth place at 295, ahead of such formidable Masters stars as Bob Charles, Roberto de Vicenzo, Tony Jacklin, Bobby Nichols, Arnold Palmer, and Lee Trevino. Palmer fell off to a dreadful 81 on his last round after being in moderate contention with a 70–75–74 start for a 219 total at the third round mark. This was the worst round Arnold had ever played in 18 Masters tournaments. All the contestants were bothered by gusty winds and difficult pin placements on very slick, close-cut greens.

Frank Beard shooting at the sixteenth as Billy Casper waits.

Henry Longhurst, veteran British golf commentator, on his TV tower.

George Archer, former Masters champion, at the fourth tee.

Jack Nicklaus out of a bunker.

Powerful Tom Weiskopf tees off at the first hole.

Billy Casper: a wedge to the green.

The magnificence of the thirteenth green.

Jim Jamieson, a rookie, being congratulated at the eighteenth for his fine showing; he finished in a tie for fourth in 1972.

Jack Nicklaus being congratulated by Charles Coody, 1971 champion, before donning new Masters coat.

Mr. Clifford Roberts about to present the 1972 trophies. Note bas relief miniature of permanent trophy awarded to winner.

43
The Major Tournament Records of the Masters Champions

BEN HOGAN: Masters 1951, 1953, U. S. Open 1948, 1950, 1951, 1953, P.G.A. 1946, 1948, British Open 1953. Total major championships, 9.

JACK NICKLAUS: Masters 1963, 1965, 1966, 1972, U. S. Open 1962, 1967, 1972, P.G.A. 1963, 1971, British Open 1966, 1970. Total major championships, 11. U. S. Amateur 1959, 1961.

ARNOLD PALMER: Masters 1958, 1960, 1962, 1964, U. S. Open 1960, British Open 1961, 1962. Total major championships, 7. U. S. Amateur 1954.

GENE SARAZEN: Masters 1935, U. S. Open 1922, 1932, P.G.A. 1922, 1923, 1933, British Open 1932. Total major championships, 7.

SAM SNEAD: Masters 1949, 1952, 1954, P.G.A. 1942, 1949, 1951, British Open 1946. Total major championships, 7.

BYRON NELSON: Masters 1937, 1942, U. S. Open 1939, P.G.A. 1940, 1945. Total major championships, 5.

GARY PLAYER: Masters 1961, U. S. Open 1965, P.G.A. 1962, 1972, British Open 1959, 1968. Total major championships, 6.

BILL CASPER: Masters 1970, U. S. Open 1959, 1966. Total major championships, 3.

RALPH GULDAHL: Masters 1939, U. S. Open 1937, 1938. Total major championships, 3.

CARY MIDDLECOFF: Masters 1955, U. S. Open 1949, 1956. Total major championships, 3.

JACK BURKE: Masters 1956, P.G.A. 1956. Total major championships, 2.

DOUG FORD: Masters 1957, P.G.A. 1955. Total major championships, 2.

HENRY PICARD: Masters 1938, P.G.A. 1939. Total major championships, 2.

CRAIG WOOD: Masters 1941, U. S. Open 1941. Total major championships, 2.

44

A Hole-by-Hole Description of the Course*

Hole No. 1, 400 Yards, Par 4, "White Pine."

This hole can be played straight away from tee to green, although the fairway does expand on the right as it approaches the green. Ordinarily, the fairway bunker on the right presents no problem for the tournament player. With a heavy wind against, however, as often happens, a half-hit tee shot may catch this bunker.

At the same time, a drive down the right side of the fairway is only important when the wind is behind and the hole is cut immediately behind the bunker at the left front of the green. Under these circumstances, the drive down the right side makes it possible for the player to play more nearly for the pin with his second shot.

The player who drives down the left side must play his second either over the bunker or into slopes that tend to direct his ball off the right side of the green.

A sort of shelf across the back of the green offers several interesting pin locations, especially when the wind is against. With the flag far back, the player thinks twice before he goes boldly for the pin and often leaves himself a very difficult approach putt from the lower level.

Notes on Hole No. 1

Sunday, April 14, 1968, was Roberto de Vicenzo's 45th birthday; and when he holed his second shot for an eagle 2 at the start of his last round of 1968, the entire gallery sang, "Happy Birthday, Roberto, Happy Birthday to you!" This was the round which "tied" him for the lead but Roberto lost because of an incorrectly totalled scorecard.

In 1970, Takaaki Kono scored an eagle 2 on his second round. He ended with 68 on the round and finished in a tie for thirteenth in the tournament, a fine showing on his first appearance in the Masters.

* The following commentaries (not including the notes on each hole) are by Robert Tyre Jones, Jr., and are quoted with the kind permission of Augusta National Golf Course and Doubleday and Company, coming from materials supplied to the press and public, *Spectators Suggestions for the Masters Tournament* by Robert Tyre Jones, Jr., and Augusta National Golf Club.

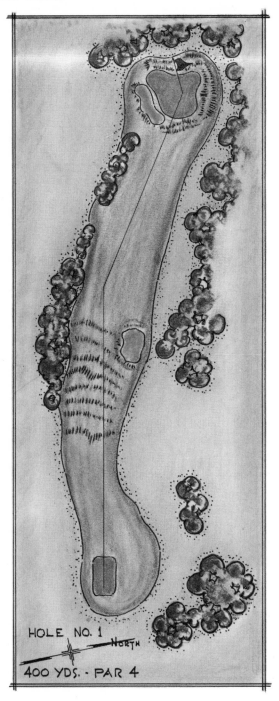

HOLE NO. 1

NORTH

400 YDS. - PAR 4

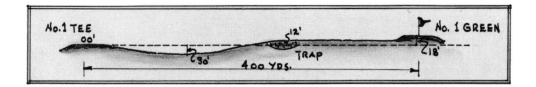

No. 1 TEE
00'

12'
TRAP

No. 1 GREEN

30'

18'

400 YDS.

Hole No. 2, 555 Yards, Par 5, "Red Dogwood."

Although this is the longest hole of the course, a well-hit tee shot will take a good run down the fairway as it slopes over the hill. One of the guiding principles in building the Augusta National was that even the par fives should be reachable by two excellent shots. The possibility of using the down slope off the tee shot brings this long hole into this category.

The contours of the fairway and the mounds at the top of the hill were constructed for the very purpose of aiding the player to make use of the slope in order to gain length. But to do so, he must drive accurately across the big bunker. If he should wander slightly to the right, the opposite face of the mound will turn his ball down the right side of the fairway and so increase the length of the hole. A drive too close to the corner is likely to kick abruptly into a most unpleasant place.

After a fine tee shot, a second played over or just past the bunker at the right front of the green may finish quite near the hole if it is placed on that side. With the flag located behind the left-hand bunker, the second shot, if played for the green, should be aimed for the center of the putting surface, in the hope of getting down in two putts for a birdie four.

Notes on Hole No. 2

In Jack Nicklaus's record-tieing score of 64 in the 1965 Masters, he drove into the right-hand pine trees on his tee-shot, came out through an opening in the pines 105 yards from the green, pitched to 22 feet from the hole, and then sank his putt for a birdie 4 on the hole, the first of eight birdies in that round.

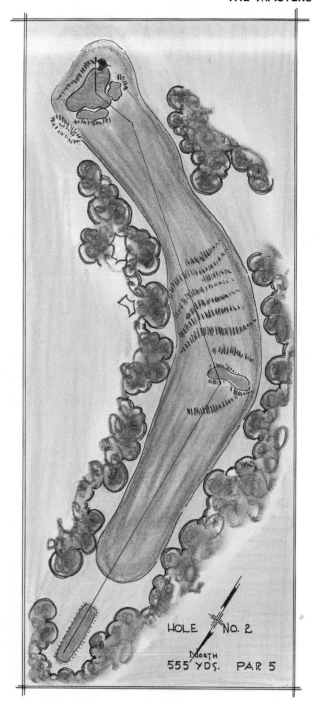

HOLE No. 2

NORTH

555 YDS.   PAR 5

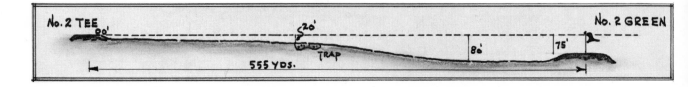

No. 2 TEE   20'   No. 2 GREEN
        80'   80'   75'
                    TRAP
                555 YDS.

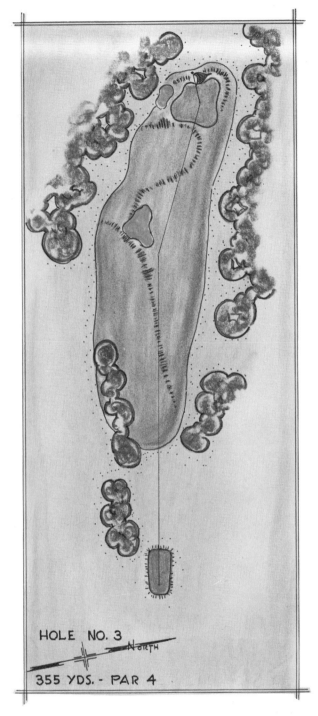

HOLE NO. 3

355 YDS. - PAR 4

Hole No. 3, 355 Yards, Par 4, "Flowering Peach."

The aim here should be slightly right of the center of the fairway onto the high ground, which gives good visibility of the green and also provides the best angle of approach to any flag location. A tee shot pulled to the left side of the fairway is very likely to follow the run of the ground into the big bunker.

The green on the left is very shallow; on the right side, it is very deep but slopes away from the player so that it is not easy to be certain of the exact location of the flag. The main problem presented by the second shot, which is normally played with a wedge or 8-iron, is to gauge the distance precisely. With the pin on the left a second shot played either short or over leaves a very difficult pitch to be made which almost always results in the loss of one stroke, often two. With the wind behind, the wise player will play for the center or left-center of the green, hoping to get down in two putts for a par four.

Notes on Hole No. 3

In the final round of the 1940 Masters, Olin Dutra, National Open Champion of 1934, "dubbed" four straight shots on this hole, scored a 6 on the way to an outgoing nine-hole score of 42. He came back in 32 on the back nine for a 74 and third place in the tournament.

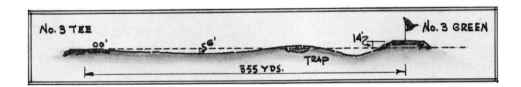

Hole No. 4, 220 Yards, Par 3, "Palm."

This hole can be varied a great deal, depending upon whether the back tee or the rear portion of the forward tee is used. From the back tee the shot is usually a strong iron or even a 4-wood or 3-wood. At tournament time there is very often a heavy wind on this hole directly against or quartering off the right. With the pin immediately behind the bunker or on the high ground at the back of the green, a precise judgment of distance is required to avoid either a long, difficult approach putt or an exacting chip.

The green is so large that a shot played to the outer reaches more often than not will result in a bogey. The back tee is somewhat elevated so that the shot is exposed to the violence of any wind which may be blowing. On certain days the wind will place many players in the left-hand bunker or beyond.

Notes on Hole No. 4

This quotation taken from the "2nd Annual Invitation Tournament Year Book of April 4, 5, 6, 7, 1935 of Augusta National Golf Club" gives these comments of architect Dr. Alister MacKenzie concerning the 4th hole:

"This is a very similar hole to the famous Eleventh (Eden) at St. Andrews. There have been scores of attempted copies of this famous hole but there is none that has the charm and thrills of the original. Most copies are failures because of the absence of the subtle and severe slopes which create the excitement of the original hole, and also because the turf is usually so soft that any kind of a sloppy pitch will stop. Previous failures, followed by, comparatively speaking, increasing successes may have given us sufficient experience to warrant us in hoping that here at last we may have constructed a hole that will compare favorably with the original."

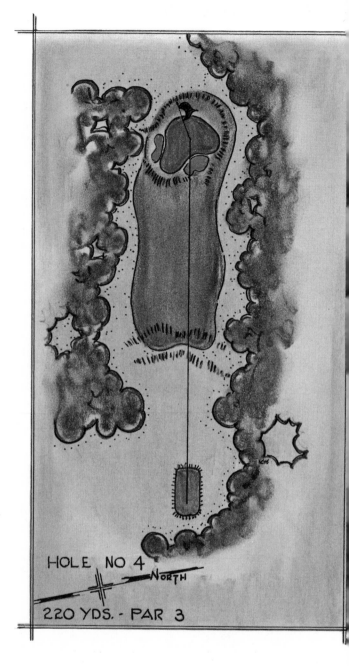

HOLE NO 4
NORTH
220 YDS. - PAR 3

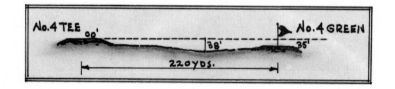

No. 4 TEE   No. 4 GREEN
220 YDS.

Hole No. 5, 450 Yards, Par 4, "Magnolia."

The proper line here is as closely as possible past the bunker on the left side of the fairway. It is not necessary to carry this bunker in order to direct the drive into a groove in the fairway on top of the hill. But it is a very comforting safety factor to have sufficient length for the carry should the shot be pulled slightly. The bunker and the woods to the left of it usually represent disaster.

Players lacking the confidence to play along the dangerous line sometimes become overcautious and play down the right side of the fairway. From this side the second shot becomes much longer and far more difficult.

On this hole, with the green's surfaces in proper condition, the second shot must be dropped short and allowed to run up. The bunker in back of the green was placed there not for penalty, but as an effort to minimize the loss from an overplayed second. Without the bunker such a shot would run far down the slope and cause the recovery to be much more difficult.

Notes on Hole No. 5

In 1956, when Cary Middlecoff, defending champion, lost by two strokes to Jack Burke, Jr., it might be said that he lost it on this hole by taking four putts.

HOLE NO. 5

NORTH
450 YDS. - PAR 4

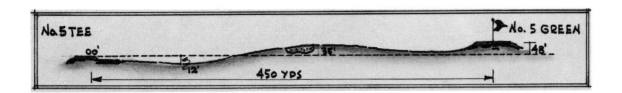

No. 5 TEE   No. 5 GREEN
00'   48'
12'   450 YDS

Leland "Duke" Gibson shows off his "hole-in-one" club.

Notes on Hole No. 6

The program of the Augusta National Golf Club "First Annual Invitation Tournament" made the claim that Hole No. 15 (Now Hole No. 6) "surpasses the original 'Redan' at North Berwick, Scotland." Bernard Darwin in his famous book *The Golf Courses of the British Isles* had this to say about the "Redan." "The 'Redan' is a beautiful one-shot hole on the top of a plateau, with a bunker short of the green to the left and another further on to the right, and we must vary our mode of attack according to the wind, playing a shot to come in from the right or making a direct frontal attack."

Aces have been scored on this hole by Leland Gibson in the first round of the 1964 Masters, by Billy Joe Patton in the fourth round of the same tournament, and by Charles Coody in the first round of the 1972 Masters.

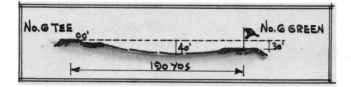

Hole No. 6, 190 Yards, Par 3, "Juniper."

The really difficult pin area here is formed by the plateau at the right back corner. To land upon and hold this plateau, the shot must be very accurately struck. With the ball left either short of this area or to the left, the first putt is extremely difficult. The front of the green immediately behind the bunker is the easiest location. Back of this, the side slope is severe. This is one of the easiest holes on the course, but the setting of the big green is very lovely when viewed from the elevated tee. This area, encompassing the sixth hole and the spectacular sixteenth is one of the most popular spectator spots.

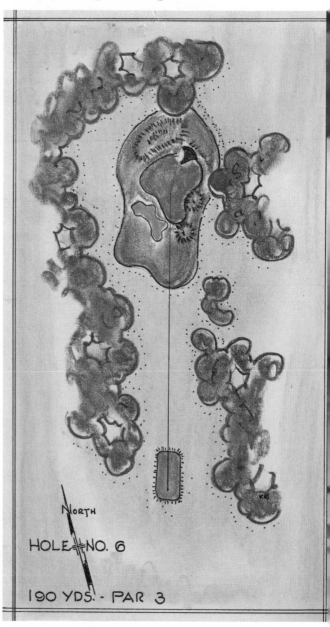

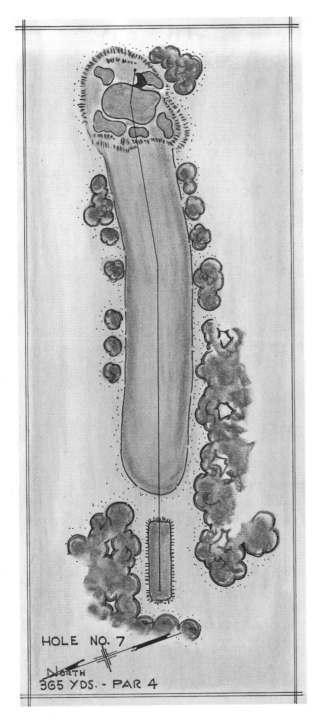

HOLE NO. 7
North
365 YDS. - PAR 4

Hole No. 7, 365 Yards, Par 4, "Pampas."

The tee shot on this hole becomes tighter year by year as the pine trees on either side of the fairway continue to spread. Length is not at a premium here, but the narrow fairway seems to have an added impact because it suddenly confronts the player when he has become accustomed to the broad expanses of the preceding holes.

Actually, the second shot is somewhat easier if it can be struck firmly so that the needed backspin may be obtained. The green is quite wide, but also very shallow. The second shot is normally a steep pitch, often with a wedge, and precise judgment of range is required. This fairway is kept in the best possible condition so that the players will uniformly encounter good lies that will produce controlled shots.

Notes on Hole No. 7

When Byron Nelson won the Masters in 1937 he set a new course record of 66 on opening day. In that round he drove the seventh green, 340 yards away. At that time the green was lower than it is today and the entrance or "tongue" was wider. The hole now plays at 365 yards.

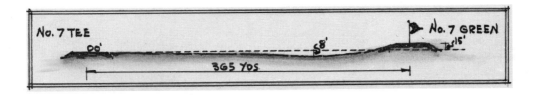

No. 7 TEE   No. 7 GREEN
00'   5'8'   15'
365 YDS

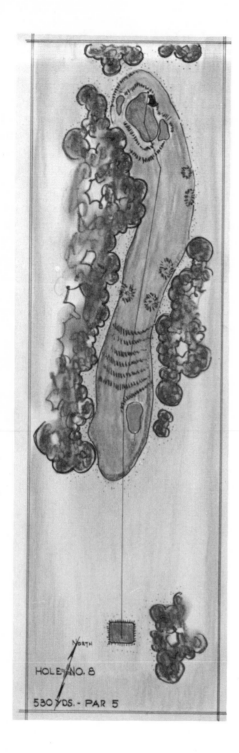

HOLE NO. 8

530 YDS. - PAR 5

Hole No. 8, 530 Yards, Par 5, "Yellow Jasmine."

This is another par five which can be reached under normal conditions with two fine shots. Here again, although the line is not directly over the bunker, it is well to hit the tee shot with sufficient power to make the carry. It is important that the ball be kept a bit to the right of the center of the fairway so that the second shot may be played through the saddle formed by the mounds at the top of the hill and so directly toward the green. Should he play left to avoid the bunker, the player must skirt the trees on the left with his second shot in order to get very near the green. Many good rounds have been spoiled by encounters with the trees at this point and a second played out safely to the right leaves a very difficult approach.

Originally there were no bunkers surrounding this green. It has been completely redesigned and rebuilt for the sole purpose of providing better visibility for spectators and a better gallery flow through what had been a congested area.

Notes on Hole No. 8

The second double eagle in Masters history was scored by Australian Bruce Devlin on the first day of the 1967 tournament. Bruce hit a 290-yard long drive and then used a 4-wood. He could not see the green from his position in the fairway. The ball hit just in front of the green, took a big bounce onto it, rolled toward the cup, hesitated on the front lip and then dropped in. His score on the round was 74 and he eventually finished at 290, tied for tenth place, on scores of 74,70,75 and 71.

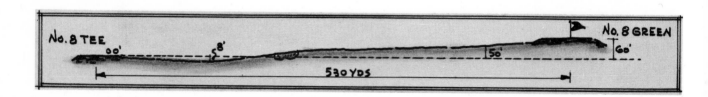

Hole No. 9, 420 Yards, Par 4, "Carolina Cherry."

This is a slight dogleg to the left which invites the player to skirt the trees on the left side. Actually, this is a delusion, because it is only with a strong wind against that this line has any advantage. The player is thus called upon to make use of local knowledge and good judgment and to resist the temptation to play close to the corner simply because the dogleg is presented. Under normal conditions, a long drive straight down the middle will give the best result since it will reach a reasonably flat area and provide an open shot for at least half the green. The hole opens up more and more as the drive is played to the right, but the distance becomes longer.

Notes on Hole No. 9

Henry Picard, Masters Champion of 1938, tells this anecdote: "Bob Jones played in the Masters tournaments until 1948. For many years it was customary for him to play with the previous year's winner. So, I played with him in the 1939 Masters. His second shot on the 9th hole went just over the back edge of the green, a couple of feet onto the short fringe. I said to him, "I'll bet you the club-house you can't keep your chip-shot on the green!" He scoffed at me. His chip rolled down the green and right off the front of it. The next year the green was flattened out."

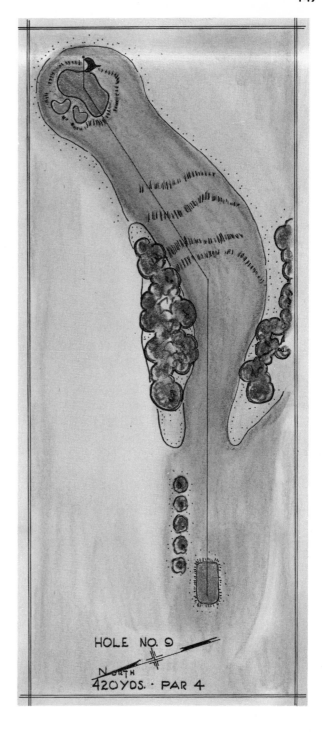

HOLE NO. 9
NORTH
420 YDS. · PAR 4

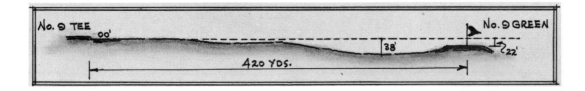

Hole No. 10, 470 Yards, Par 4, "Camellia."

This, to my mind, is one of the most beautiful holes I have ever seen, especially at tournament time when the dogwood and redbud are in bloom. The tee is on high ground and, I might add, immediately in front of my cabin. The fairway goes down in a broad slope from the tee, following on the left a straight line to the green; but on the right, it fans out to a considerable width. On the right side, the fairway continues in the same general slope to the bottom of the hill just short of the green. But on the left at about 230 yards from the tee, the slope runs off abruptly into a valley of fairway some 30 or 40 yards wide. Since the hole is of good length for a par four, it is decidedly advantageous for the player to make use of the run offered by this slope. Therefore, the line of play is down the left side as closely as one may dare.

A tee shot played to the right which does not avail itself of the slope will add at least two club numbers to the length of the second shot, in addition to which the approach to the green must be made across the slopes, rather than directly into them. A good drive down the left side usually makes it possible to play the second with a medium iron, sometimes even less if the wind is behind.

The green nestles on a hillside and is framed by some giant pines which give the impression of Gothic spires, and the wooded areas all around are rich in dogwood and redbud. When the dogwood is in bloom, one gets the impression a snowstorm has recently occurred.

Notes on Hole No. 10

In the 1940 Masters, a three-putt here by Lloyd Mangrum was the only error he committed in a nine birdie round of 64, the course record which stood until 1965 when Jack Nicklaus tied it.

In the Snead-Hogan playoff of 1954 which Snead won (70–71) this hole was the scene of a dramatic exchange of scores when Snead apparently headed for a bogey to go one stroke behind, holed a 65-foot chip shot from the back of the green to go one stroke ahead.

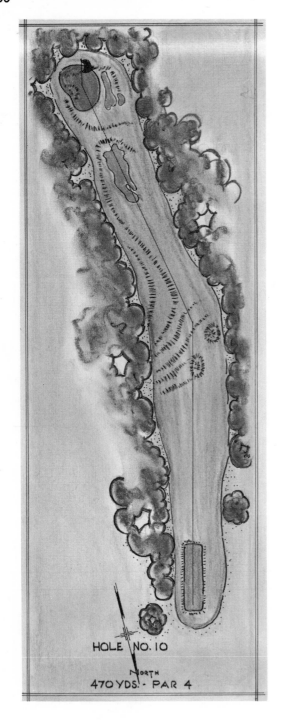

HOLE NO. 10

NORTH
470 YDS. - PAR 4

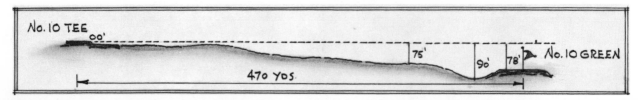

No. 10 TEE 00'   75'   90'   78'   No. 10 GREEN

470 YDS.

Hole No. 11, 445 Yards, Par 4, "White Dogwood."

The tee shot to this hole is blind in that the fairway upon which the ball is to land is not visible from the tee. Nevertheless, the limits of the fairway are sufficiently well-defined by the trees on either side. A drive down the left side of the fairway provides better visibility of the forward portions of the green, but slightly to the right of center is better should the pin be located on the promontory of the green extending into the water hazard on the left. The pin location on this projection of the green is often reserved for the final round of the tournament.

The second shot is usually played with a 3-iron or a stronger club, and a player must be bold and confident indeed to go for the pin when it is in this location. A second shot played into the water here must be dropped on the near bank, with water still intervening between the player and the hole. Too much daring here can easily cost a seven or an eight.

With the pin located at any place on the green other than the left-hand projection, the hole appears simple. Yet it has a puzzling difficulty. Should the pin be at the back of the green, the player tends to let up on his second shot for fear of the severe penalty involved in overplaying. Often he leaves himself an approach putt of more length than he would like. With the pin on the forward area of the green, a shot underplayed may bound to the left and come dangerously close to the water. A great many players play this hole safely to the right, relying on getting a long putt or chip dead for the par.

Notes on Hole No. 11

This green was originally to the right of its present position. However, in the opinion of Henry Picard, 1938 Masters Champion, the hole was just as difficult then as it is today.

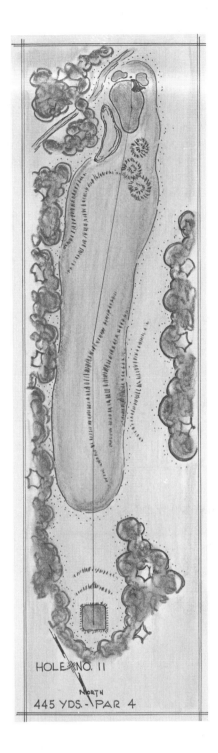

HOLE NO. 11

445 YDS. - PAR 4

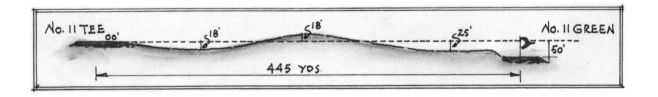

No. 11 TEE   00'   18'   18'   25'   No. 11 GREEN   50'

445 YDS.

Hole No. 12, 155 Yards, Par 3, "Golden Bell."

The championship location for the pin here is in the shallow area of the green on the right. Here the distance must be gauged very accurately and the wind sweeping down Rae's Creek is often deceptive to the player standing on the tee. The inclination here is to be well up, or to favor the left side where the green is wider. To play safely to the left is simple, but the putting problem which results is not easy. Pin locations on the left side of the green can be made testing only by pushing them far forward or far back. If the tee shot has been played into the creek, the short pitch to the shallow green is terrifying indeed.

Notes on Hole No. 12

Aces have been scored on this hole by William Hyndman, III, in 1959 and Claude Harmon in 1947.

Lloyd Mangrum is said to have called this hole "the meanest little hole in the world."

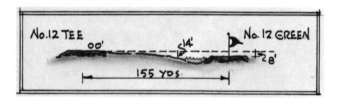

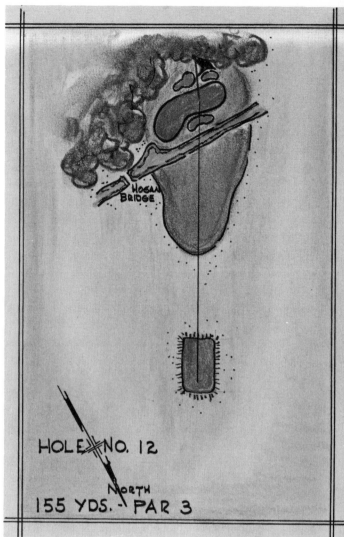

Hole No. 13, 475 Yards, Par 5, "Azalea."

Number ten at 470 yards is a par four because of the favorable slope of the ground offered to the tee shot. However, thirteen is a par five, because under certain conditions of wind and ground few players will risk trying for the green with a second shot. In my opinion this thirteenth hole is one of the finest holes for competitive play I have ever seen. The player is first tempted to dare the creek on his tee shot by playing in close to the corner, because if he attains his position he has not only shortened the hole, but obtained a more level lie for his second shot. Driving out to the right not only increases the length of the second, but encounters an annoying sidehill lie. Whatever position may be reached with the tee shot, the second shot as well entails a momentous decision whether or not to try for the green. With the pin far back on the right, under normal weather conditions, this is a very good eagle hole, because the contours of the green tend to run the second shot close. The chief danger is that the ball will follow the creek.

The most difficult pin locations are along the creek in the forward part of the green. A player who dares the creek on either his first or second shot may very easily encounter a six or seven at this hole. Yet the reward of successful, bold play is most enticing. Several tournaments have been obviously won and lost on holes twelve and thirteen. Others, upon careful analysis, will be seen to have been won or lost here, even though the decision may not have been obvious at the time.

This hole is a splendid example of what can be done by taking advantage of natural features. The splashes of sand in the woods behind the green and the azalea along the left side were placed there in order to add beauty to the natural setting.

Notes on Hole No. 13

In the 1968 Masters Don January hit his drive "around the corner" of the thirteenth hole and then put a 3-iron on the green near the back fringe, 60 feet away from the cup. He then putted off the green into the downslope of Rae's Creek. It was said that this was the first time in Masters's history that anyone had done this. January chipped the ball back and scored a 6.

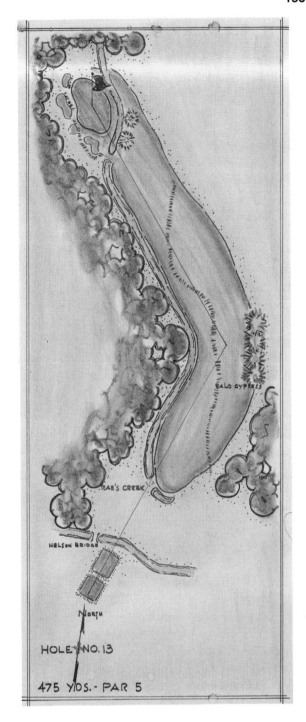

HOLE NO. 13

475 YDS. - PAR 5

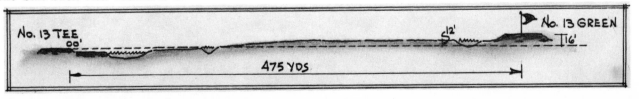

Hole No. 14, 420 Yards, Par 4, "Chinese Fir."

This is another hole whose innocent appearance can be deceiving. The most popular line off the tee is slightly to left of center, to gain the crest of the hill and risk the runoff of the fairway to the right. A slight deviation to the left of this line often encounters the upper branches of the small group of pine trees on this side.

A drive straying off to the right leaves the player on lower ground from which his ability to see the left side of the green is completely obstructed by a large mound in the middle of the fairway.

The green is quite large and with many interesting and difficult contours. A mound in back protects against overrunning the left side of the green, but no such buffer exists on the right. The putting surface along the front of the green spills over the contours into the fairway. But an approach putt from this area is exceedingly difficult. A really good second shot leaving the ball close to the hole is most comforting.

Notes on Hole No. 14

This hole is of the Scottish type often requiring a carefully placed run-up shot to hold the green. It is similar in character to the 6th hole at famous St. Andrews.

Hole No. 15, 520 Yards, Par 5, "Fire Thorn."

The fairway of this hole is quite wide. The short rough on the left is far removed from the line of play and there is no demarcation on the right between the fairway of the fifteenth and that of the seventeenth. The tee shot may be hit almost anywhere without encountering trouble.

It is nevertheless of considerable importance that the line of play be along the crest of the hill, a little to the right of the center of the fairway. This fairway, being on high ground, usually provides more run to the ball than most other holes of the course. It is also more exposed to the effect of any wind which may be present. Two tees, front and back, are provided so that the length may be adjusted within wide limits according to playing conditions.

The design of the green causes it to be most receptive to a second shot played from the right-center of the fairway. The greater depth of the putting surface is on the right side. The left side is quite shallow, considering the length of the second shot, and the most severe hazards lie on this side. A ball played over the green on this side may very well run down into the pond at the sixteenth hole. More often than not, it is the better part of wisdom to play the second for the main body of the green, even though the hole may be cut on the left side. When Gene Sarazen holed his second shot with a three wood for his famous double eagle, the hole was cut near the back of the green. Gene's ball landed on the tongue of the green in front and rolled directly into the cup.

Under almost any conceivable conditions the second shot to this hole suggests precarious possibilities. With the wind against, the player must decide whether his power and the state of the game warrant an effort to reach the green. With a following wind he may have to consider whether he will be able to hold the green, even though it might be well within reach. Billy Joe Patton's magnificent bid to be the first amateur to win the Masters ended when he tried to reach this green from the rough on the left. The ball finished in the pond. The resulting six was one too many. Had he played safely for a five, he would have tied with Snead and Hogan.

The only bunker on the hole was placed there just a few years ago, not so much as a feature of play, but to protect spectators occupying the mound on this side. Without the bunker, players uncertain of their ability to reach the green were using this area as a sort of haven for the second shot. Now they either play directly for the green or, quite frankly and safely, short of the pond.

Notes on Hole No. 15

The spectator's view of this hole either from behind the hole or from the rough along the right hand side of the fairway is one of the most exciting on the course in order to experience the drama of the players' decisions whether or not to "go for the green" with the second shot.

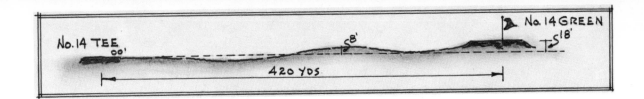

No. 14 TEE
00'

S8'

No. 14 GREEN

S18'

420 YDS

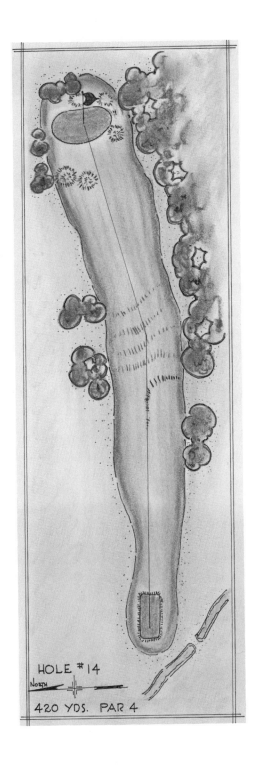

HOLE #14

NORTH

420 YDS. PAR 4

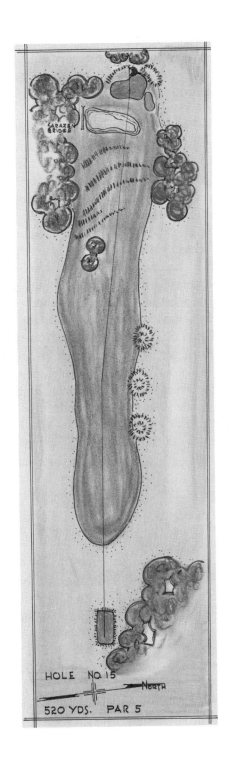

GRAZEN BRIDGE

HOLE NO. 15

NORTH

520 YDS. PAR 5

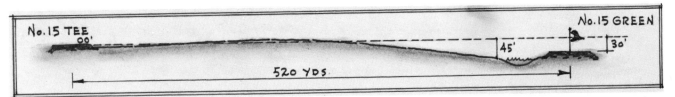

No. 15 TEE
00'

No. 15 GREEN

45'

30'

520 YDS

Hole No. 16, 190 Yards, Par 3, "Red Bud."

The tee shot to this hole will be played by the tournament players with a number two, three, or four iron, depending upon the wind. The pond extends from the front of the tee very nearly to the edge of the green. The contours of the green are such that several pin locations can be found along the left side close to the bunkers and the pond. This is also the low side, so that a tee shot played for the middle of the putting surface, but with a slight draw, can be made to curl down toward the hole. This, of course, involves risk that the draw may be overdone, landing its perpetrator in the sand or water. A shot played straight to the flag over water and sand must be very accurately adjusted for length. Pin locations on the right side may vary from an acceptable one in the V-shaped front of the green through a crown about halfway back, from which the ball may be expected to fall off to the left, back to a gently gathering area at the rear. This latter area will provide a good opportunity for a birdie to a player who has hit an accurate tee shot. With the pin on this side, the threats come from the bunkers on the right and the runoff of the green toward the left.

Apart from the visible hazards on this hole, the player who leaves his ball on the forward area of the green with the pin near the back can have quite a problem getting down in two putts. Three putts on this green sealed Hogan's defeat by Snead in the 1954 playoff.

Notes on Hole No. 16

Ray Billows scored a hole-in-one "on the fly" on this hole in the Masters of 1940. The hole played at 145 yards at that time. He used a wedge for the shot. Willie Goggin also aced this hole in the tournament of 1934. Other aces were scored by Ross Somerville in 1934, John Dawson in 1949 and Clive Clark in 1968.

Bert Yancey made 2 on this hole eight times in nine consecutive rounds in 1967, 1968, and the first round of 1969.

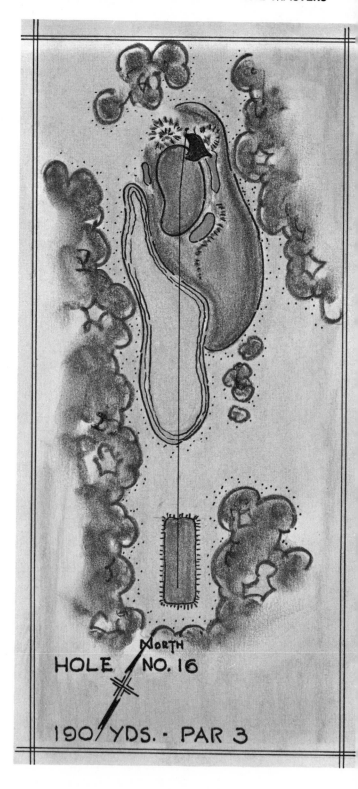

HOLE NO. 16

190 YDS. · PAR 3

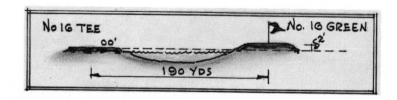

No 16 TEE   No. 16 GREEN
00'   52'
190 YDS

Hole No. 17, 400 Yards, Par 4, "Nandina."

The pine tree in the fairway, although only a little more than a hundred yards from the tee, has grown to such proportions that it provides a real menace to the tee shot. The proper line of play is to the right of this tree, but also to the left of the big mounds and two other trees at the top of the hill. Depending upon the wind, a fine drive may leave a second shot of anything from a good 5-iron or easy 4 to a short pitch. To become involved with the mounds on the right may impose difficulties of either lie or visibility, or both.

On the left side the green slopes gently, but quite perceptibly, from front to back. With a following wind, therefore, even the shortest pitch over the bunker and the slopes off the base of the mound must be played quite accurately. A ball played too strongly to this side of the green may take a good run off a slope at the back and so leave a difficult return chip. On the right side, immediately behind the bunker, there is a nice little basin which provides a most inviting place for the pin on quiet days. On this side, the green slopes very definitely upward toward a sort of plateau area near the back. This is a very difficult pin location when the wind is against, because a shot played boldly to get near the hole is likely to go over the green, down a considerable slope, whereas the less bold shot must leave some very difficult putting to do.

The hole looks innocuous enough, yet it provided the decisive moments in the 1956 tournament when Jack Burke, in a stretch run against Ken Venturi and Cary Middlecoff, scored a birdie three at the hole, while Venturi took five and Middlecoff six. Burke won by one stroke over Venturi and two over Middlecoff.

Notes on Hole No. 17

This hole has been both cruel and kind to Arnold Palmer. In 1959, when he was defending champion he missed a two footer here which cost him his chance to catch Art Wall, Jr. However, in 1960 he holed a 35-footer for a birdie and then followed with a 6-foot birdie on No. 18 to edge Ken Venturi out of first place.

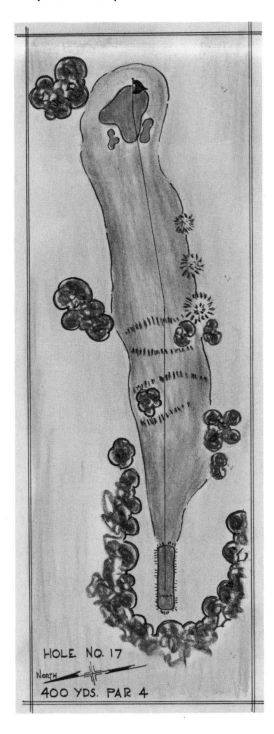

HOLE NO. 17
North
400 YDS. PAR 4

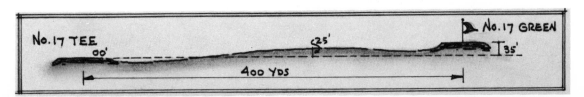

No. 17 TEE　　　　　　　　　25'　　　　　　No. 17 GREEN
00'　　　　　　　　　　　　　　　　　　　　　　35'
|— 400 YDS —|

Hole No. 18, 420 Yards, Par 4, "Holly."

This hole is a slight dogleg to the right. The bend in the fairway comes at the top of a hill that can just about be carried by a fine tee shot. The bunker at the left front of the green causes it to be of some importance to drive close to the trees up the right side of the fairway, or even, if possible, to bend the tee shot a bit around the corner.

The front area of this green is nicely molded to receive a pitch and provide a good putt for a birdie when the hole is cut here. Yet a ball driven to the left side of the fairway safely away from the trees must be pitched quite closely over the guarding bunker. Behind this friendly area the putting surface slopes upward to the middle of the green. A second shot played up this slope even a dozen feet past the hole can very easily result in three putts. It was from just such a position that Ben Hogan three-putted to lose by one stroke to Herman Keiser in 1946. In 1958 both Doug Ford and Fred Hawkins tried and missed similar putts to tie Arnold Palmer.

This eighteenth green is quite long. The rear one-quarter of the putting surface embraces a plateau area which is often used as a pin location. The great difficulty here is to be up without going over. A second shot played into the slope in the middle of the green either stops or rolls back, so that the ensuing putt is difficult indeed.

In the 1957 tournament Doug Ford avoided all these putting difficulties by holing a full blast from the bunker in front of the green to give him a winning margin of three strokes.

Notes on Hole No. 18

In 1957 when Doug Ford holed out his explosion shot for a birdie three from the front bunker he exclaimed, "My God, that's the best shot I ever made."

It undoubtedly was. He won with 283 to Snead's 286.

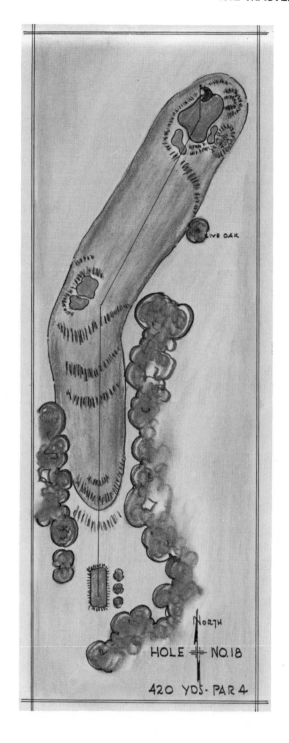

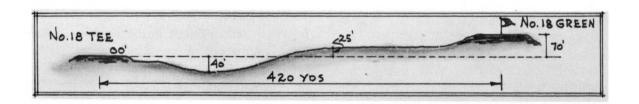

45
A Final Word

Overall, the Augusta National is not intended to be a punishing golf course. It is, however, a course which under tournament conditions (that is, with the green surfaces firm and keen) severely tests the player's temperament. The difficult greens demand fierce and unremitting concentration and determination. When the golf course is wet and the wind quiet, it is easy. We always hope it will not be that way during the first week in April.

ROBERT T. JONES, JR.